The Politics of Ballot Design

US federalism grants state legislators the authority to design many aspects of election administration, including ballot features that mediate how citizens understand and engage with the choices available to them when casting their votes. Seemingly innocuous features in the physical design of ballots, such as the option to cast a straight ticket with a single checkmark, can have significant aggregate effects. Drawing on theoretical insights from behavioral economics and extensive data on state ballot laws from 1888 to the present, as well as in-depth case studies, this book shows how strategic politicians use ballot design to influence voting and elections, drawing comparisons across different periods in American history with varying levels of partisanship and contention. Engstrom and Roberts demonstrate the sweeping impact of ballot design on voting, elections, and democratic representation.

Erik J. Engstrom is Professor of Political Science at University of California, Davis. He is the author or co-author of three books – most recently *Race, Class, and Social Welfare: American Populism since the New Deal* (2020). He was the co-winner of the 2015 J. David Greenstone Prize for best book in Politics and History from the American Political Science Association.

Jason M. Roberts is Professor of Political Science at University of North Carolina at Chapel Hill. He is the author or co-author of three books, including *The American Congress* (2019) *and Ambition, Competition, and Electoral Reform* (2013).

The Politics of Ballot Design

How States Shape American Democracy

ERIK J. ENGSTROM
University of California, Davis

JASON M. ROBERTS
University of North Carolina at Chapel Hill

CAMBRIDGE
UNIVERSITY PRESS

University Printing House, Cambridge CB2 8BS, United Kingdom

One Liberty Plaza, 20th Floor, New York, NY 10006, USA

477 Williamstown Road, Port Melbourne, VIC 3207, Australia

314-321, 3rd Floor, Plot 3, Splendor Forum, Jasola District Centre, New Delhi - 110025, India

103 Penang Road, #05-06/07, Visioncrest Commercial, Singapore 238467

Cambridge University Press is part of the University of Cambridge.

It furthers the University's mission by disseminating knowledge in the pursuit of education, learning and research at the highest international levels of excellence.

www.cambridge.org
Information on this title: www.cambridge.org/9781108822633
DOI: 10.1017/9781108904254

© Cambridge University Press 2020

This publication is in copyright. Subject to statutory exception and to the provisions of relevant collective licensing agreements, no reproduction of any part may take place without the written permission of Cambridge University Press.

First published 2020
First paperback edition 2022

A catalogue record for this publication is available from the British Library

ISBN 978-1-108-84280-8 Hardback
ISBN 978-1-108-82263-3 Paperback

Cambridge University Press has no responsibility for the persistence or accuracy of URLs for external or third-party internet websites referred to in this publication, and does not guarantee that any content on such websites is, or will remain, accurate or appropriate.

To Mary and Emma
EJE

To Sarah
JMR

Contents

List of Figures		*page* ix
List of Tables		xi
Acknowledgments		xii
1	Introduction	1
	1.1 States and Election Law	4
	1.2 Plan of the Book	7
2	How the Ballot "Nudges" Voters	15
	2.1 Introduction	15
	2.2 Ballot Architecture	16
	2.3 Nudging Voters	23
	2.4 Implications for Candidates	29
	2.5 Ballot Architecture over Time	30
	2.6 Are Ballot Architects Aware?	34
3	Ballot Architecture in the Progressive Era	37
	3.1 Introduction	37
	3.2 From Party Ballots to Secret Ballots	38
	3.3 California	43
	3.4 New York	48
	3.5 Maryland	49
	3.6 The Political Logic of Ballot Architecture	53
	3.7 Implications for Ballot Roll-Off	55
	3.8 Implications for Turnout	57
	3.9 Conclusion	58

4		The Personal Vote Era, 1940–2000	59
	4.1	Introduction	59
	4.2	Ohio: Saving "Mr. Republican"	61
	4.3	Connecticut: The Power of Defaults	65
	4.4	North Carolina	69
	4.5	Patterns of Change	70
	4.6	The Incumbency Advantage	73
	4.7	Representational Style	80
	4.8	Conclusion	90
5		Ballot Architecture in the Contemporary Partisan Era	92
	5.1	Michigan	97
	5.2	North Carolina	108
	5.3	Comparing Michigan and North Carolina	120
	5.4	Iowa and West Virginia	122
	5.5	Conclusion	127
6		Reconsidering the American Ballot	130
	6.1	The Consequences of Ballot Design	130
	6.2	The Causes of Ballot Design	132
	6.3	Scholarly Implications	135
	6.4	Policy Implications: Designing a Better Ballot	137

Bibliography   142
Index   149

Figures

1.1	Straight ticket voting and African-American population, North Carolina, 2012	page 3
1.2	Party column ballot	7
1.3	Office bloc ballot	8
2.1	Palm Beach County butterfly ballot	17
2.2	Alabama Senate special election, 2017	19
2.3	German Reichstag election ballot, 1938	20
2.4	Ballot with party box	26
2.5	Party ballot, North Carolina, 1868	27
2.6	Ballot type by State, 1888–2008	32
3.1	Example of a ballot poster	41
3.2	Roll-off by ballot type, California	48
3.3	Roll-off by ballot type, New York	50
3.4	Roll-off by ballot type, Maryland	52
3.5	Seats/votes curve by ballot type, 1888–1940	54
4.1	Relationship between governor and US Senate election, Ohio, 1944	64
4.2	Relationship between governor and US Senate election, Ohio, 1950	65
4.3	Roll-off by party lever rule, Connecticut	67
5.1	"Hanging" chad	93
5.2	"Pregnant" chad	94
5.3	Correlation between presidential and US House vote, 1872–2016	96

5.4	Straight-ticket voting and African-American population, Michigan, 2012	99
5.5	Straight-ticket voting and African-American population, Michigan, 2014	100
5.6	Straight-ticket voting and African-American population, Michigan, 2016	101
5.7	Straight-ticket voting and ballot roll-off, Michigan, 2012	104
5.8	Straight-ticket voting and ballot roll-off, Michigan, 2014	105
5.9	Straight-ticket voting and ballot roll-off, Michigan, 2016	106
5.10	Proposal 3 and roll-off in Michigan, 2018	108
5.11	Obama vote and straight-ticket voting, North Carolina, 2012	109
5.12	Roll-off and straight-ticket voting, North Carolina 2012	110
5.13	North Carolina roll-off change, 2012–2016, by straight-ticket voting	114
5.14	North Carolina turnout difference, 2012–2016, by straight-ticket voting	115
5.15	Effect of straight-ticket voting ban on change in roll-off, 2012–2016	122
5.16	Straight-ticket voting and ballot roll-off, Iowa, 2016	124
5.17	Straight-ticket voting and roll-off, West Virginia, 2014	126
5.18	Straight-ticket voting and roll-off, West Virginia, 2018	127
5.19	West Virginia roll-off change, 2012–2016	128

Tables

3.1	Partisan change in state ballot laws, 1888–1940	*page* 53
3.2	Effects of ballot type on roll-off and turnout, 1888–1940	55
4.1	Partisan change in State ballot laws, 1940–2000	71
4.2	Effect of ballot type on roll-off, 1956–2000	72
4.3	Estimating the direct and quality effect of incumbency	76
4.4	Estimating the "Scareoff" effect of incumbency	77
4.5	Ballot type and split-ticket voting	78
4.6	Ballot type and bill sponsorship	84
4.7	Ballot type and legislative effectiveness	86
4.8	Ballot type and presidential support	89
5.1	Ballot roll-off in Michigan, 2014, 2016, and 2018	107
5.2	Straight-ticket voting and wait time at the polls, North Carolina, 2014	112
5.3	Straight-ticket elimination and turnout in North Carolina, 2016	116
5.4	Ballot order and the 2016 North Carolina Supreme Court election	119

Acknowledgments

This book began as a purely historical project that combined our mutual interest in political history and institutional change. Both of us had coauthored work that analyzed the effect of the adoption of the Australian ballot in the late nineteenth and early twentieth centuries, and Roberts had done some preliminary work on the effects of the ballot in the post–World War II era. This mutual interest led us to the natural questions of why states changed their laws surrounding ballot type and what the political dynamics of these changes were. While we were working on this project, current events intervened. North Carolina's election reform efforts in 2013 combined with changes in Michigan, Iowa, and West Virginia added a contemporary angle to our research and allowed us to explore how the dynamics of ballot law changes work in modern American politics. To complete this project we had to collect a large amount of data on ballot laws and election results. Much of our data collection was funded by a grant from the National Science Foundation, SES-1060978. We also benefited from the research assistance of many individuals, including Brice Acree, Austin Bussing, Emily Cottle, Michael Greenberger, Ryan Freeman, Nick Howard, Caitlin Jewitt, Nathan Pinnell, and Ryan Williams. We offer special thanks to Emily Cottle for indexing the manuscript.

Our work has also benefited from comments received from various friends and scholars over the past few years. We thank John Aldrich, Jim Curry, Gerald Gamm, Mary Ellen Gurewitz, Jason Kelly, June Speakman, Wendy Schiller, Charles Stewart, Sarah Treul, and seminar participants at the University of Virginia, the University of Chicago, Vanderbilt University, the Ohio State University Moritz School of Law, the University of North Carolina, and Duke University for their helpful comments on earlier portions of this work. Rachel Raper was instrumental in helping us understand the dynamics of the 2016 North Carolina Supreme Court contest.

Roberts would like to thank Steve Roberds for encouraging him to pursue a career in political science rather than the high school classroom and Steve Smith for being the best advisor and mentor a person could ask for. He would like to thank his colleagues at the University of North Carolina for providing a collegial and intellectually stimulating environment. Finally, he would like to express gratitude to his family. Sarah Treul is an amazing scholar, mother, wife, and best friend. Her capacity to love, show patience, provide encouragement, and manage the logistics of life is boundless. Roberts dedicates this book to her. Our children, Eleanor and Catherine, brighten every day. Witnessing their daily joy of discovery provides both a welcome diversion from work and inspiration to continue engaging in the research enterprise.

Engstrom would like to thank his faculty and staff colleagues at the University of California, Davis. They made it possible to finish this book while also tending to administrative duties. He would also like to thank his family for their support. My wife, Mary, and daughter, Emma, provided constant love and encouragement. This book is dedicated to them.

Portions of this work appeared in Erik J. Engstrom and Jason M. Roberts, 2016. "The Politics of Ballot Choice," *The Ohio State Law Journal* 77 (4):839–865, and are reprinted here with permission.

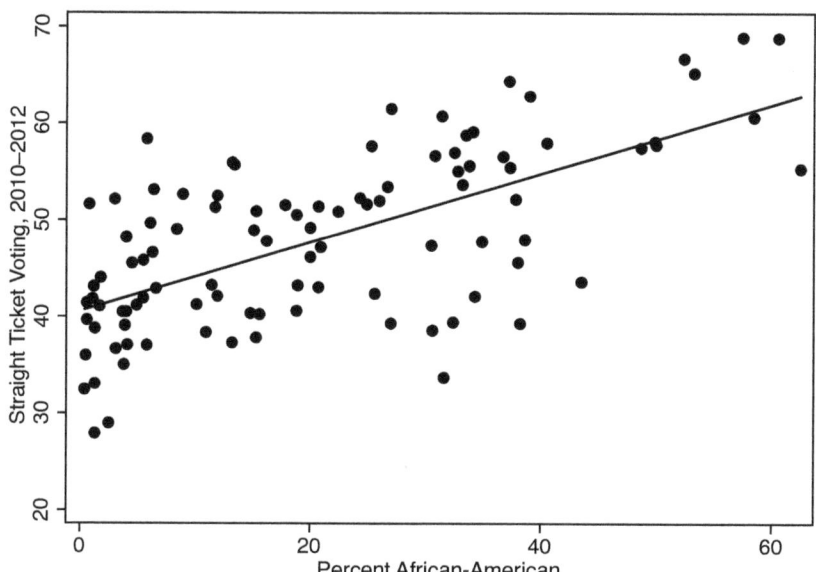

FIGURE 1.1 Straight ticket voting and African-American population, North Carolina, 2012

Note: Data drawn from the North Carolina State Board of Elections and the US Census Bureau. Dots represent North Carolina counties, line is a bivariate regression line.

findings in political science is that increasing the cost of voting decreases turnout (Brady and McNulty 2011). The elimination of the STV option increased voters' costs in at least two ways: (1) it took longer to fill out a ballot, and (2) it produced longer lines and hence deterred turnout as potential voters went home rather than waiting in a long line.

Both of these effects worked to bolster the Republican Party's tenuous grip on power in North Carolina. Despite their electoral victories in 2010 and 2012, Republicans were still outnumbered by Democrats in registered voters by more than 800,000 and had every reason to believe that competition for statewide offices would continue to be fierce.[4] Barack Obama and Mitt Romney had won the state electoral votes in 2008 and 2012, respectively, by the narrowest of margins. By designing an electoral reform that decreased the likelihood of turnout for the opposing party's most reliable voters, North Carolina Republicans were attempting to insulate themselves from defeat in the event that partisan tides

---

[4] In 2016, Governor McCrory was defeated by Democrat Roy Cooper by a margin of 10,277 votes out of more than 4.7 million cast.

turned ever so slightly against them. Then Buncombe County Republican Chairman Don Yelton defended the Act against charges of racial bias on Comedy Central's "The Daily Show"[5] by admitting its partisan intent, stating in part that lawmakers had not used racial motives in enacting reform, rather the law was designed merely to "kick Democrats in the butt."

For many, the North Carolina case might seem puzzling. The enormous body of political science scholarship on elections typically argues that votes are determined by objective factors such as issues, economic conditions, or candidate qualities. Ballot formats are often considered innocuous parts of the background, not directly influencing votes much less the decision to vote at all. But in the case of North Carolina we see an instance where election outcomes were, at least in part, determined by the structure of the ballot. Was the case of North Carolina post–2012 unique or has ballot design played a more important role in electoral politics than conventional wisdom would have us believe?

As we demonstrate in this book, the strategic manipulation of ballot architecture like what occurred in North Carolina is not new. Party politicians in state legislatures have used ballot design for political gain at least since the advent of the secret ballot in the late nineteenth century. Moreover, the consequences of alterations to ballot architecture have, at times, been immense. In this book, we combine and analyze decades' worth of data to demonstrate that ballot design can affect who votes, how they vote, and how representatives choose to carry out their job in the legislature.

1.1 STATES AND ELECTION LAW

The ability of citizens to choose the individuals that represent them through the act of voting is one of the fundamental features of a democratic form of government. The vote is the linchpin that holds the relationship between the government and the governed together. Though most adherents of a democratic form of government hold voting rights as a core democratic value, fewer people give a great deal of thought to *how* citizens vote in a democracy and how variation in how people vote can affect election outcomes. We contend that this is an oversight. The

---

[5] The show originally aired on October 23, 2013.

form and structure of the ballot presented to voters can affect who votes and how those who choose to vote cast their ballots.

Not only that, but the form and structure of the ballot are not exogenously determined. Rather it is strategic political actors – typically partisan majorities in state legislatures – who serve as the primary architects for ballot laws. We typically think of elections as taking place within a stable set of ground rules about the design and structure of ballots. Yet as we demonstrate in this book, the ballots themselves are often the subject of political contestation and manipulation.

What makes this potentially problematic in the US is that the states are granted broad powers to set electoral laws by Article I, §4 of the US Constitution, which states that "The Times, Places and Manner of holding elections for senators and representatives, shall be prescribed in each state by the legislature thereof; but the Congress may at any time by law make or alter such regulations, except as to the places of chusing senators." This clause sets up a system of shared federalism between the states and the federal government. Congress can and does set national standards from time to time, but many aspects of how elections are conducted are decided directly by state legislatures and local governments.

The system of electoral federalism has clear consequences for how voters experience democracy. Some of these are undoubtedly positive, as states are able to introduce and experiment with electoral institutions that facilitate voting such as vote by mail, automatic registration, and an early voting period (Springer 2014). In addition, widely decentralized election administration makes it much more difficult for nefarious actors to hack or otherwise interfere with elections on a national scale. However, many of the consequences have been unquestionably negative. The decades-long Jim Crow regime in the American South violently suppressed the voting rights of the region's African-American citizens.

Electoral federalism also opens the door for partisan majorities in states to potentially shape election practice in ways that benefit themselves. As a result, how voters experience voting varies considerably depending on where one lives. States vary widely on factors such as closing date for registration, ease of absentee voting, early voting, and as we focus on in this book, the design of the ballot. The variation is far from random. In fact, it is often the product of fierce partisan competition for control of government and, as a result, the machinery of elections. This creates a system whereby winning parties can, under certain conditions, compete under, construct, and change the rules of electoral democracy as they see fit.

To be clear, we do not contend that the design of the ballot directly prevents someone from voting, nor do we contend that it changes a voter's preferences over candidates, but we present considerable evidence that it can and does serve as a "nudge" that shapes how some voters use the ballot (Thaler and Sunstein 2008).

1.1.1 Ballot Types

American states face two broad design choices in constructing electoral ballots. The first is whether to organize the ballot by party or by office. The former are called "party column" ballots and they are designed with all candidates for a particular party listed under the party's name and often include a large party symbol (see Figure 1.2). The latter are called "office bloc" ballots and they are designed with all candidates for a particular office listed under the name of each office on the ballot (see Figure 1.3). The second choice is whether or not to provide a partisan selection device or "party box" on the ballot that would allow voters to choose all candidates for a particular party by checking a single box or pulling a lever for the voter's preferred party. These two choices combine to create four basic ballot types that we analyze throughout this book: (1) party column with party box, (2) party column without party box, (3) office bloc with party box, and (4) office bloc without party box. The office bloc ballot is associated with a higher rate of split-ticket voting than is the party column ballot (Rusk 1970). Likewise, STV is more common when the ballot contains a party box (Burden and Kimball 2002).

As we discuss in the coming chapters, ballot design efforts can have both intended and unintended consequences on election outcomes. The North Carolina change that began this chapter was meant to bolster the fortunes of the Republican Party, but as we detail in Chapter 5, it likely cost them a seat on the North Carolina Supreme Court. Likewise, Republicans in Michigan were stymied in their efforts to change ballot laws by the voters of the state, who overturned a law removing the straight-party option from the ballot and enshrined it into the state constitution (more on this in Chapter 5). However, more often than not the choice of ballot type has effectively served as an institutional solution to a fundamental problem faced by governing majorities – how to maintain power.

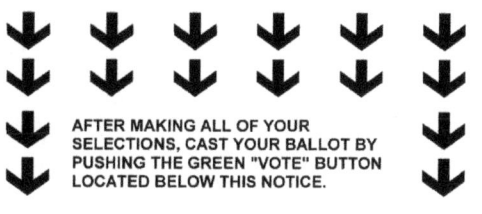

FIGURE 1.2 Party column ballot

1.2 PLAN OF THE BOOK

The goal of this book is to more fully understand the causes and consequences of ballot format changes across a broad swath of American political history. We contend that ballot laws provide political parties with an institutional solution to electoral uncertainty. To bolster this claim, we have collected a comprehensive dataset of the timing and form of ballot design changes from 1888 through the present. These data have allowed us to unpack the forces behind ballot law changes. They have also allowed us to more definitively assess the effects of ballot formats on election outcomes, party competition, and representative behavior in both the US Congress and state legislatures.

FIGURE 1.3 Office bloc ballot

The geographical focus of our book is the American states. But the book also contributes to a burgeoning scholarly literature in comparative politics that examines balloting procedures in historical and contemporary settings. One strain of scholarship looks at the historical movement from open voting to secret balloting. As we discuss in Chapter 3, the American states adopted secret balloting in the late nineteenth and early twentieth centuries. But the US was not alone. A number of scholars have recently studied the switch to secret voting during the same time period in Britain and continental Europe. Works in this historical literature have identified a dramatic alteration in the nature of voter behavior and party organization in the late nineteenth and early twentieth centuries (Aidt and Jensen 2017; Kam 2017; Mares 2015; Mares and Young 2016; Stokes et al. 2013).

Comparative politics scholars have also recently turned their attention to the consequences of ballot design in contemporary settings, with much of this research focusing on Central and South America (Barnes et al. 2017; Calvo et al. 2009; Gingerich and Medina 2013; Gingerich 2019; Katz et al. 2011; Nichter 2008; Pachon et al. 2017; Reynolds 2006). Our book draws on, and expands upon, the insights of these scholars.

1.2.1 Designing Democratic Institutions

The institutional feature of democracy we are primarily concerned with in this book is ballot design. But the rules regarding balloting touch upon larger normative questions regarding the design of democratic institutions. The central normative question underlying our book is whether politicians should be in charge of electoral rules or whether the rules should be made free from politicization? In the US, and elsewhere, politicians do not always accept institutions as they find them (Riker 1986; Shepsle 2003). In fact, much of partisan competition concerns the structure of the game itself. William Riker (1986) introduced the term "heresthetic" to capture the broad class of activities aimed at altering the rules of the game. These can take a number of different forms. Laws regarding who votes, when people vote, how they vote, and how those votes are translated into offices can each potentially determine electoral winners and losers.

Politicians have an incentive to tilt the rules to influence the terms of political competition (Anzia 2012, 2014; Bawn 1993; Benoit 2004; Boix

1999; Smith and Remington 2001). Take, for example, the history of suffrage and voting rights. Throughout much of US history politicians have attempted to alter who can and cannot participate through suffrage rules (Keyssar 2000; Valelly 2009). Sometimes the short-term calculations of party elites led to restrictions on suffrage and voting rights (e.g., Kousser 1974). But one can also find in other places and times that the strategic calculations of politicians led to significant expansions of suffrage and voting rights (e.g., Corder and Wolbrecht 2016; Harvey 1998; Keyssar 2000; McConnaughy 2015; Springer 2014). The key normative question, then, is whether we want electoral laws subject to the short-term strategic needs of politicians?

These questions also apply directly to the case of ballot formats. As we will see, politicians have strategically employed ballot laws at times for the purpose of raising the costs of voting yet at other times for expanding who can participate and making it easier to vote. We will have much more to say on these issues in the concluding chapter.

Our work makes a number of contributions to the study of elections and legislative behavior: (1) drawing on insight from behavioral economics, we develop a theory (see Chapter 2) of how seemingly minor changes to ballot design affect voter choices, (2) we analyze how and why elites change the rules that govern their elections, and (3) we analyze the major consequences of those changes on representation, the incumbency advantage, and aggregate voter turnout. Our analyses have an unusually broad scope of more than hundred years of US electoral history, which allows us to demonstrate the uncanny parallels between today's political environment and late nineteenth-century America. We are also able to combine macro-level data on all states with detailed case studies of several states across time. These case studies help illustrate our central arguments and help the reader see how our theoretical arguments play out in real-world politics.

In Chapter 2, theoretical explanation of how the format of the ballot affects the choices American voters make with regard to voting is discussed. When casting votes, we normally take the format of the ballot for granted. Yet, numerous decisions have to be made before the ballot is presented to the voters. For example, what order should the candidate names be placed? Should candidate names be listed in columns underneath party labels or should candidates be listed in office-by-office groupings? Should the ballot include party emblems? Should voters be able to select all candidates for one party by pulling a lever or checking one box? Each and every one of these decisions can influence outcomes.

The design of the ballot almost certainly will not make a hardline Republican vote for a Democratic candidate, or vice versa, but ballot design can influence whether that voter completes their ballot for all offices. Or it may influence the time it takes to fill out a ballot and thereby the lengthy lines at polling places. We contend that these seemingly small effects can add up to large electoral consequences.

Borrowing from the language of behavioral economics, we argue that the structure in which choices are presented can "nudge" voters toward certain decisions (Thaler and Sunstein 2008). We use examples from Nazi Germany, the 2000 US presidential election, and research on restaurant menus to demonstrate how the structure of choices presented to people can shape outcomes. The person, or people, responsible for making these decisions are what Thaler and Sunstein (2008) call choice architects. These architects organize "the context in which people make decisions" (Thaler and Sunstein 2008: 3). Given that the US Constitution delegates decisions concerning the "time, place, and manner" of elections to the states, this means that state legislatures are the choice architects when it comes to deciding how voters in a given state experience the fundamental feature of a democratic system of governance – voting. We then apply this theoretical structure to the major types of ballots used in the US and develop expectations as to how various ballot formats will affect election outcomes.

Given that voters have an incentive to rely on simplifying cognitive strategies – such as using information shortcuts – we contend that they are especially susceptible to the subtle impact of ballot design. For example, including a straight-ticket option on the ballot can radically simplify voting. Here a voter has the option of voting for an entire party slate of candidates by marking a single box. A straight-ticket option allows voters to reduce a series of potentially complex decisions into a single and efficient choice – vote for the entire Democratic or Republican slate. The absence of such an option can induce voter mistakes and/or discourage the voter from making a choice for all offices.

Chapters 3, 4, and 5 present the core of our empirical analysis. We have found it helpful to break the past 130 years of ballot law changes into three broad periods.[6] In Chapter 3, we set the political backdrop for understanding the causes and consequences of ballot law changes in

---

[6] These time period designations are meant primarily as a convenient way to break up the data analyses for the reader. They do not precisely match any widely agreed on period designations, but they do generally overlay with recognizable periods in American electoral history.

the late nineteenth and early twentieth centuries (1888–1940) – a period that we label broadly as the Progressive Era. The party system of the late nineteenth and early twentieth centuries was highly partisan. American elections in the nineteenth century were built on a series of exchange relationships: between voters and politicians, between politicians and party bosses, and between bosses and businesses. A core feature of this system was the highly decentralized system for conducting elections, with parties themselves printing ballots, selecting candidates, and mobilizing voters. The system featured high levels of turnout and a strong national component in elections. The winner of the presidency almost always controlled the Congress and many state legislatures.

The advent of the Australian or secret ballot upset many aspects of this system. With voters able to cast their ballots in secret for the first time, party bosses could no longer directly monitor voters. In addition, the state-printed ballot made split-ticket voting much easier for the voter. As such, the national parties could no longer count on local politicians to mobilize large numbers of voters on their behalf (Carson and Roberts 2013).

States had to then decide what form of the Australian ballot to adopt. These choices included party column or office bloc and whether or not to include a party box or symbol on the ballot. In this chapter, we demonstrate that parties adopted or changed the type of ballot they used in ways that helped the party making the change electorally. We also show in this chapter that these choices about ballot form had immense consequences for voter turnout and ballot roll-off at the state level. We provide detailed case studies of ballot changes in California, Maryland, and New York as well as an empirical analysis of voter turnout and ballot roll-off for all states from the 1888–1940 time period.

In Chapter 4, we focus on what we call the Personal Vote Era that stretches roughly from World War II to the disputed 2000 presidential election between George W. Bush and Al Gore. In this era, the strategic problem that parties face changed. As politicians become more careerist and states depended on careerists members of Congress to deliver goods and services to the state they needed to shield politicians from adverse national political tides. In doing so, we find that states changed ballot laws in ways that protected incumbents. Moreover, after the New Deal, the battle for partisan control of the Congress was not as fierce as it had been in the previous era. As such, using ballot laws to try to win national elections receded in importance. Instead, incumbents used ballot laws to protect their institutional positions.

Chapter 4 also includes detailed case studies of ballot law changes in Ohio, North Carolina, and Connecticut to illustrate the larger themes of the chapter. We also conduct comprehensive analysis of all states using district-level data. We find that certain forms of the Australian ballot (office bloc with no party box) significantly enhanced the incumbency advantage in US House elections. We are the first to present evidence that changes in state ballot laws were a major determinant of the growth of the incumbency advantage in the 1960s. These macro-level findings are further supported by individual-level data collected by the American National Election Study (ANES). We also present evidence in Chapter 4 that demonstrates that members of the US Congress have differing representational styles based on the type of ballot that they are chosen under. Members who are chosen in states with the most candidate-centered ballot forms (office bloc with no party box) introduce more bills in the House as an attempt to increase their personal vote with their constituents. They also appear to be more effective at seeing their proposals turned in public laws (Volden and Wiseman 2014).

In Chapter 5, we focus on the post–2000 era that has once again been defined by a competitive and fiercely partisan political climate. In this era – which we name the Contemporary Partisan Era – political polarization and fierce battles over majority control in Congress have returned. We argue that the extended battle over how to properly count ballots in the 2000 presidential election (*Bush* v. *Gore*) changed the dynamics of ballot reform in multiple related ways. First, it highlighted the importance of seemingly mundane election administration issues such as ballot design, voting equipment, and standards for counting ballots. This issue went from something few had ever considered to something that literally decided the outcome of a presidential election. Second, it prompted Congress to get involved in election administration in hopes of preventing another Florida fiasco. Congress in 2002 passed the Help America Vote Act (HAVA), which authorized spending up to $650 million dollars to improve poll access for voters with disabilities and upgrade obsolete voting technology in states and localities – including punch card machines. The passage of HAVA resulted in many states making changes to voting equipment and ballot type that were not directly related to partisan political goals. Finally, the razor-thin margin of the 2000 election signaled the beginning of an era of heightened partisan competition for Congress, the presidency, and many state legislatures.

In many ways, the post–2000 era mirrors the politics of the late nineteenth century. The strategic problem politicians confront is once again how to win partisan majorities at the state and national level in a polarized and electorally competitive environment. The sweeping Republican victory in the 1994 congressional elections had ended a four-decade period in which the partisan control of the US House was rarely, if ever, in doubt heading into an election year. Majority party margins have been razor-thin since 1995, and both parties have gone into almost all election cycles with a realistic chance of winning or losing majority control. At the same time, the two major parties have never produced more polarized voting records, which has made the opportunity costs of winning and losing incredibly high (Lee 2016).

A number of states, including West Virginia, Iowa, North Carolina, and Michigan, have eliminated the STV option in the past fifteen years. We provide analysis of these states with a particular focus on the cases of North Carolina and Michigan. Our results demonstrate that removal of the straight-ticket option in North Carolina suppressed voter turnout considerably in counties that had previously had high levels of STV. One of us (Roberts) served as an expert witness in the legal battle over STV in Michigan. This involvement has allowed us to secure data on STV in Michigan and allowed us access to documents demonstrating that the Michigan legislature fully understood that removing the STV option would lead to longer lines at the polls and depressed turnout in areas (largely urban) that had seen high levels of STV usage. This includes correspondence between members of the Michigan legislature and the Republican activists outside the legislature.

In Chapter 6, we summarize our findings and present conclusions from our work. In doing so we focus on the implications of our work for elections and voting in America. Our results powerfully demonstrate that the design of the ballot has had important consequences for election outcomes for most of American history and that these effects are as strong today as they have ever been. We use these findings to highlight a number of policy tradeoffs related to ballot design, including a nationalization of standards and a prohibition on elected officials directly choosing the type of ballot they will seek reelection under. While there is no perfect balloting system that could be adopted, our results can serve as a roadmap to reformers who wish to improve certain elements of American democracy.

2

How the Ballot "Nudges" Voters

2.1 INTRODUCTION

All democratic systems must select the rules and procedures that determine how citizens choose their elective officers. The casting of ballots by citizens is the heart of the democratic process. When voters arrive at the polling place on election day, or receive a ballot in the mail, they are presented with a preprinted ballot. Unbeknownst to most, the physical appearance of the ballot varies widely from state to state. When casting votes most voters may take the format of the ballot for granted, yet a number of decisions had to be made before the ballot was presented to voters. What order should the candidate names be placed? Should candidate names be listed in columns underneath party labels? Or should candidates be listed in office-by-office groupings? Should the ballot include party emblems? Should information about the candidates' prior officeholding experience, or incumbency status, be included? These are just some of the myriad decisions that have to be made prior to distributing the ballot to voters.

As we demonstrate in later chapters, each of these decisions can and does influence election outcomes. To be sure, the design of the ballot almost certainly will not make a hard-line Republican vote for a Democratic candidate or vice versa.[1] However, ballot design can influence whether that voter completes their ballot for all offices. The design of a ballot can influence the propensity of weak partisans to vote a straight-party ticket or split their vote across candidates from different parties. Ballot design can certainly influence how long it takes for a voter to fill

---

[1] Though see our discussion of the 2016 North Carolina Supreme Court contest in 2016.

out a ballot, which affects the length of lines at the polling place and the time a person must commit in order to vote in a particular election. These examples represent a small sample of the potential effects of ballot design, and while each of these effects may seem facially trivial, a major theme of our work is that these seemingly small effects can and do have substantial electoral consequences.

2.2 BALLOT ARCHITECTURE

We begin by examining how ballot design can influence voter decisions. The overall framework we adopt is to consider voting as involving both costs and benefits. Unlike most consumer decisions, the act of voting for a single individual is a low-cost, low-benefit activity (Aldrich 1993). On the cost side of the ledger, scholars have long argued that voting is relatively low-cost for most people most of the time. The costs include not only the expenses incurred for registration and going to a polling station (or dropping a ballot in the mail) but also the efforts put into gathering information about candidates. But on the whole scholars argue that these activities require only a modest amount of effort for most (Niemi 1976). On the benefit side the impact of a single vote on deciding who wins or loses an election is infinitesimally small in most elections. While a voter may receive a psychological or symbolic boost from voting for the candidate of their choice, the individual vote will have little material impact on the outcome.

Thus, the decision about whether to vote or not is what John Aldrich (1993) calls a "low-cost, low-benefit activity." As a result, small changes in either the costs or the benefits can have a profound effect on individual behavior. In the language of behavioral economics, the structure in which choices are presented can "nudge" decision-makers toward an outcome (Thaler and Sunstein 2008).[2] The small details of design can affect outcomes. For example, the structure and layout of items on a restaurant menu can influence the likelihood a customer will choose particular items; as such, restaurant managers often place their highest margin dishes at the center/right of a menu. The person, or people, responsible for making these architectural decisions are what Thaler and

---

[2] There is a stream of behavioral economics research that attempts to explain human behavior that is facially irrational, such as failing to sign up for employer-provided retirement benefits, which is not our focus here. Rather, our focus is on how ballot design choices can alter the choice context for voters or would-be voters.

2.2 Ballot Architecture

Sunstein (2008) call "choice architects." These choice architects affect outcomes by organizing "the context in which people make decisions."

One path through which choice architecture can influence outcomes is by facilitating, or failing to prevent, human error (Herrnson et al. 2012). A political example comes from the infamous case of the butterfly ballot in Palm Beach County, Florida, during the 2000 presidential election. As can be seen in Figure 2.1, the ballot was laid out with the candidate names appearing on a left page and right page. In the middle were punch holes that were supposed to line up with the candidate names. Voters were asked to punch the hole that lined up with the candidate they were voting for. George W. Bush voters had it comparatively easy. They simply had to match the first name on the left side of the ballot, Bush, with the first punch hole.

Al Gore supporters, however, faced a more daunting physical task. They had to match the second name on the left side of the ballot, Gore, with the third punch hole in the center of the ballot. This design made it easy for Gore voters to mistakenly vote for Pat Buchanan. Buchanan's name was listed on the right-hand side of the ballot, slightly below Bush's name and above Gore's. The most comprehensive research on the effects of this ballot design concluded that it likely cost Gore the election (Wand et al. 2001).

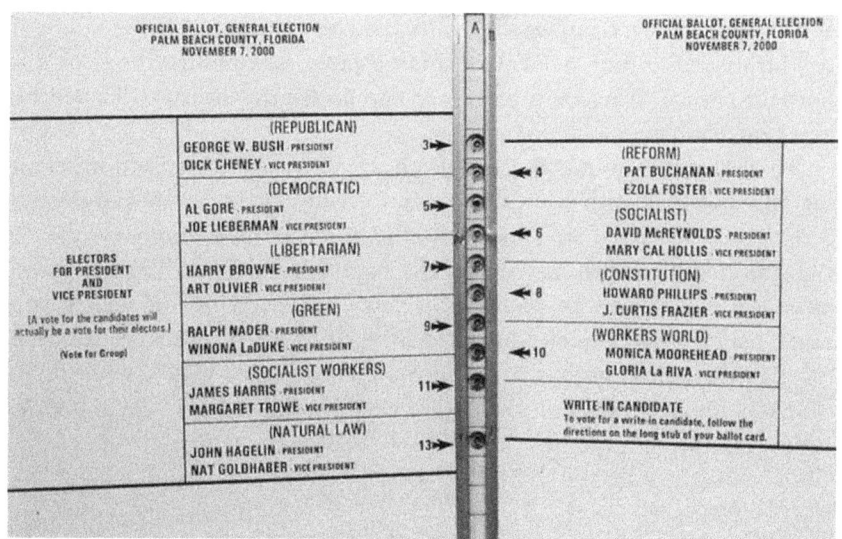

FIGURE 2.1 Palm Beach County butterfly ballot

In addition, the ballot included the instructions "vote for group." A number of voters mistook this to mean "punch two holes," punching separate holes for both a presidential and a vice presidential nominee. As a result, a number of voters may have over-voted by mistakenly punching holes for both Gore and Joe Lieberman, or two holes for Bush and Dick Cheney. The Palm Beach butterfly ballot is a clear example where design – in this case, poorly thought-out design – interacted with the innate human capacity for error to produce an unintended outcome (Kimball and Kropf 2005; Sinclair and Alvarez 2004).

Design also affects how simple or complex a task may be to complete. When choices are simple people tend to gather sufficient information to make a reasoned decision. With a small number of choices it is easier to assess the alternatives and weigh the various trade-offs. Thaler and Sunstein (2008) use the example of a person choosing an office at a new job versus choosing an apartment in a new city. In choosing an office at a new job, an employee is usually presented with a small number of options.[3] In this case it is fairly easy to weigh the differing attributes of the offices (e.g., size versus view) and come to a decision. In choosing an apartment in a new city, one must take a much larger number of factors into consideration. The chooser needs to take into account the neighborhood quality, school districts, the location of the apartment relative to their workplace and transit, whether or not the apartment has a gas range, the wine selection at local bars, as well as a host of other factors. When choices are complex, humans tend to rely on simplifying cognitive strategies. When faced with a large range of options, the details of how the choice structure is presented can nudge the decision (Thaler and Sunstein 2008).

An electoral example of a simple choice structure is an election featuring only one race with two candidates. Consider the 2017 special election Senate race in Alabama. This election featured a single contest with only two candidates. Figure 2.2 shows the ballot. In this instance, the voter's attention is likely to be focused on this single election. In such a situation ballot nudges likely mattered little, if at all. There were no other races to distract attention from the Senate race. As a result, voter attention was focused solely on the choice between Roy Moore (R) and Doug Jones (D).

---

[3] Our experience in academia suggests that the number is often one!

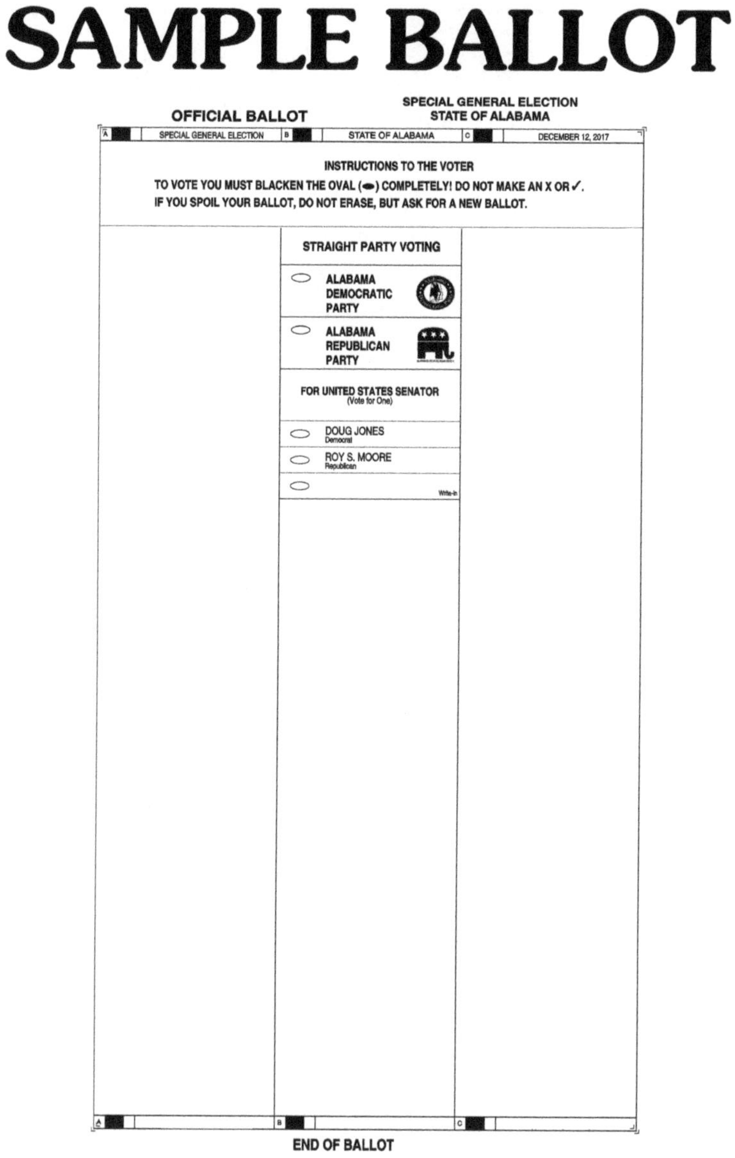

2.2 Ballot Architecture

SAMPLE BALLOT

OFFICIAL BALLOT	**SPECIAL GENERAL ELECTION** **STATE OF ALABAMA**

SPECIAL GENERAL ELECTION	STATE OF ALABAMA	DECEMBER 12, 2017

INSTRUCTIONS TO THE VOTER

TO VOTE YOU MUST BLACKEN THE OVAL (⬤) COMPLETELY! DO NOT MAKE AN X OR ✓.
IF YOU SPOIL YOUR BALLOT, DO NOT ERASE, BUT ASK FOR A NEW BALLOT.

STRAIGHT PARTY VOTING

○ ALABAMA DEMOCRATIC PARTY

○ ALABAMA REPUBLICAN PARTY

FOR UNITED STATES SENATOR
(Vote for One)

○ DOUG JONES
  Democrat

○ ROY S. MOORE
  Republican

○ _____ Write-in

END OF BALLOT

FIGURE 2.2 Alabama Senate special election, 2017

However, even in cases with a seemingly simple binary decision, strategic choice architects may still use ballot design to try and nudge voters. A vivid, and disturbing, example comes from Nazi Germany. The

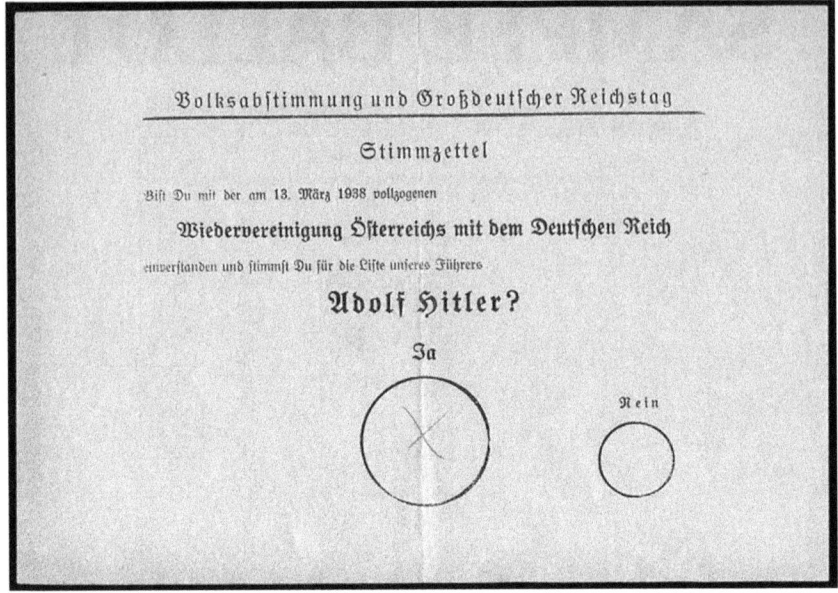

FIGURE 2.3 German Reichstag election ballot, 1938

parliamentary elections to the Reichstag, held in 1938, took the form of a simple referendum. The question given to voters was whether or not to approve a single list of 813 Nazi candidates to the Reichstag. To be sure, it is unlikely that most voters in this totalitarian regime needed a ballot nudge to vote the way the dictatorship wanted. But the ballot architects took no chances (see Figure 2.3). The ballot presented the yes option (*ja*) in a giant circle in the middle of the ballot, while the no option (*nein*) was relegated to a smaller circle in the corner. Such a nudge might make a difference for a voter who could not read or serve as a visually chilling warning to any wavering voters.[4]

As choices become more complex humans respond by adopting simplifying strategies. An example of a complex decision might be choosing among various medical treatments for a serious illness. Research has found that patients are prone to following the first course of action suggested to them upon learning of the diagnosis (Thaler and Sunstein 2008). Of course, the first course of action may not always be the best option. Thus, as choices become more complex, humans seek

---

[4] The results were 99.01 percent *ja*, 0.91 percent *nein*, and 0.08 percent of the ballots were invalid.

out simplifying strategies and, in doing so, become more prone to the influence of design nudges.

When voters have to make decisions across multiple offices – like in a presidential election year – they are also faced with a potentially complex set of choices. Voters might be asked to make decisions about offices ranging from the president to Congress, to state legislatures, to municipal offices, to school boards, to various referenda and amendments. Those jobs differ considerably. They require different talents and skill sets. The job of a president is unlike that of a state agriculture commissioner or a county coroner.[5] The skills necessary to succeed in each job are quite different. What a voter wants out of each office may also differ. The more offices on the ballot, the larger set of candidates about which voters must make decisions.

Consider planning for a major house renovation. To complete a renovation, a homeowner might need to hire a plumber, electrician, roofer, carpenter, and painter, among others. Each of those jobs requires a particular set of skills and talents. Hiring decisions require applying a different set of criteria across the multiple decisions. What makes a good plumber may well be different from what makes a good roofer. Hiring separately for each job, therefore, presents homeowners with a mind-boggling set of logistical challenges. Not only does one have to choose high-quality tradespeople, but one must arrange them to do work in a certain order (i.e., sheetrock should be finished before the painters arrive). Transaction costs are sure to be high, and the potential for agency loss is real. One way to simplify the process is to outsource these decisions to a general contractor whose job it is to subcontract and coordinate these separate activities. The homeowner's decision is now boiled down to a much simpler cognitive task: hire a competent general contractor.

Elections in some important respects present a more challenging cognitive task. In a home renovation there is a clear mapping of choices to individual welfare – it is probably safe to blame the plumber you chose for the leaking pipes. Similarly, in medical decisions there is often a direct connection between a person's choices and their subsequent welfare. The chosen course of treatment will have a direct effect on the person making the choice – the patient. Similarly, consumer decisions, such as purchasing

---

[5] Candidates, however, may try to gain voters by taking positions that, while popular with the electorate, are likely irrelevant for the job they are seeking. One of the authors observed a candidate for coroner in a rural Alabama county advertising, apparently without irony, that he was "pro-life."

a boat, also have a clear mapping between the individual making the decision and their personal welfare. There is also an immediate opportunity cost to an individual in making a consumer purchase. The money spent to purchase a boat cannot also be spent on concert tickets. This direct relationship between individual choices and personal welfare creates a heightened incentive to pay close attention to how those choices affect well-being and to choose options that are likely to maximize utility.

In elections it is much harder to map individual choices to outcomes. When a voter casts a ballot, all they are literally doing is marking a piece of paper, pulling a lever, or pushing a button on a computer screen. That action is then combined with similar actions by numerous other individual actors to produce an outcome. The outcome a voter receives from voting in, say, a presidential election is contingent on the decisions of millions of other people. As a result, the gap between the action of marking a ballot and the subsequent outcome of a government is immense. Whether a voter pulls the Democratic or Republican lever, or simply does not vote, will have essentially no impact on the outcome of the election (Downs 1957). As a result, the opportunity cost of marking one option on a ballot over another option or not voting at all is negligible (Aldrich 1993). This radically decreases the incentives people have to gather meaningful information about candidates and their platforms and to participate at all. We all endure the repetitive filling out of forms on clipboards and irregular waiting times in medical offices because we expect to receive tangible benefits from the treatment received; voting, on the other hand, offers a minimal relationship between effort expended and benefits gained (Aldrich 1993).

Just as homeowners can simplify their choices by choosing a general contractor, voters also have a compelling incentive to simplify their decision-making. For example, a large literature in political science has shown that one way voters simplify their decisions is by relying on a candidate's party affiliation (Campbell et al. 1960; Hetherington 2001). Knowing that a candidate is a Democrat or Republican provides a fair degree of information to a voter about how a candidate will behave in office even if the voter is ignorant of the details of that candidate's platform or background. Similarly, voters have also been shown to use the simple shortcut of whether or not the candidate is an incumbent (Carson et al. 2007; Cox and Katz 1996; Erikson 1971).

Because voters have an incentive to rely on simplifying cognitive strategies – such as using information shortcuts – they are especially susceptible, we contend, to the subtle impact of ballot design. Our argument is that the process of voting can be nudged by the architecture of the ballot. For example, including a straight-ticket option on the ballot can radically simplify voting. Here a voter has the option of voting for an entire party slate of candidates by marking a single box. A straight-ticket option allows voters to reduce a series of potentially complex decisions into a single and efficient choice – vote for the entire Democratic or Republican slate.

Another example of ballot architecture is the order in which candidate names are presented. Such a seemingly innocuous design choice should be irrelevant if voters assess the qualities of candidates one by one. But we also know that voters weigh the cognitive costs of voting against the benefits of being fully informed. As we will see with the North Carolina Supreme Court example in Chapter 5, the choice architecture of ordering the names of candidates on the ballot can have a profound effect on election outcomes.

One study found that being listed first increased a candidate's vote percentage by an average of 2.5 percent (Miller and Krosnick 1998). Another study used the natural experiment provided by California's ballot order rules. Between 1978 and 2002, the names of candidates in California statewide races were listed on the ballot in a randomized order. Being listed first mattered in primary races and in nonpartisan races. In nonpartisan races, being listed first increased a candidate's vote share by three percentage points (Ho and Imai 2008).

A similar study examined primary elections in New York City, which also randomizes name order on the ballot. This study found that being listed first had a pronounced effect on vote shares (Koppell and Steen 2004). In other words, ballot order seems to matter most in races where voters cannot rely on a party label to provide an informational shortcut.

Subtle design choice, such as name order, can nudge voters toward an outcome. These nudging effects can be especially pertinent for voters facing situations where they have little information – such as down ballot races or nonpartisan races.

2.3 NUDGING VOTERS

Most nudging is sold positively. The presidential administration of Barack Obama, for example, instituted a Social and Behavioral Science team inside the White House in order to help government work more efficiently and help people make better decisions. Efforts ranged from getting students to show up for their first year of college, to insurance enrollment, to getting employees to print documents double-sided. Many were quite successful, such as the double-sided printing reminder, while others such as persuading doctors to prescribe fewer opioids were less successful. The efforts, however, were transparent and pursued goals that were not particularly controversial.

Choice architects may not always have the best interests of end users in mind, however. Businesses, for example, are profit-driven. At the end of the day they only make money if they sell or resell products to customers at a price that is greater than the costs of obtaining and producing the product. This profit motive may or may not coincide with creating a choice architecture that serves the best interest of their customers. This is why the authors do not order fish on Mondays.[6]

Much like business owners, politicians are self-interested and take actions that further those interests. A primary goal of most politicians is to gain and retain elected office (Mayhew 1974). There are, of course, many ways to pursue this goal, but as we demonstrate in later chapters one method they use to further this goal is to select a ballot format that enhances their electoral interests. Their chief goal is to win elections, which may or may not correspond to designing a voting process that is efficient or easy to navigate for voters.[7]

Throughout this book we analyze the overall format of the ballot – whether the ballot should be organized in a party column or office bloc format, and a closely related decision as to whether the ballot should include a straight-ticket provision or not. For the last roughly 130 years these formatting decisions have almost always been made by

---

[6] As Bourdain (2000) points out, most restaurants receive seafood shipments on Tuesday and Friday of each week. Ideally, all of the Friday order would be sold by the close of business on Sunday, but if product remains it is often fashioned into a well-priced "special" that is placed prominently on the menu on Monday. Bourdain notes that in addition to being at least four days old, the Monday "special" fish may or may not have been kept at proper temperature throughout the weekend rush.

[7] It is also worth mentioning another important class of actors: local and state election administrators. There is a substantial literature on the technology of voting (Stewart III 2011). This literature examines important issues relating to matters like whether to use optical scanners or written ballots, where best to put polling place locations, the impact of early voting and mail-in ballots, etc. The administrators involved are primarily interested in improving the election experience for voters while at the same time ensuring a fair and accurate vote. In this book we are not centrally concerned with these aspects of election administration.

state legislatures and written into state electoral codes. This makes state legislators the primary architects of ballot formats.

The most basic ballot distinction in American elections is between the party column ballot, which lists each party's candidates for each office in a column on the ballot (see Figure 1.2) and the office bloc ballot, which lists the candidates for each office on ballot by office (see Figure 1.3). In addition, some ballot formats provide a box at the top allowing voters to simply cast a straight ticket with one check mark (see Figure 2.4).

An additional important design feature is whether party emblems are allowed at the top of the ballot. The inclusion or exclusion of party emblems mattered more in places and historical periods with lower literacy rates (Figure 2.5 provides an early example). The inclusion of a party emblem provided an easy visual clue for illiterate voters or voters not fluent in reading English. Given the high level of literacy rates in the contemporary US, the presence or absence of a party emblem probably matters little for voters these days, but in the early to mid-twentieth century such visual cues might be critical to election outcomes in certain parts of the country. Literacy rates in the early twentieth century were significantly lower among certain ethnic groups with restricted access to educational opportunities – most notably African Americans and recent immigrants (Valelly 2009).

For a voter who could not easily read candidate names, the party emblem provided a design solution to make it easier for these voters to cast a ballot. This of course produced fights among state legislators over whether to include party emblems on the ballot. Those politicians with support among groups with lower literacy rates had an incentive to push for the inclusion of party emblems. Democrats in Maryland, for instance, removed party emblems from the ballot in 1901 with the express aim of making it more difficult for African Americans and poor whites to vote (Callcott 1986).

2.3.1 Split-Ticket Voting

A key decision that a voter must make when casting his or her ballot is whether or not to vote for all candidates of one party or to split his or her votes among more than one party. Before the advent of the Australian ballot, it was quite difficult for voters to cast a split ticket, as they had to physically remove one name from the ballot and replace it with another often with the help of a "paster." With the new ballot listing candidates

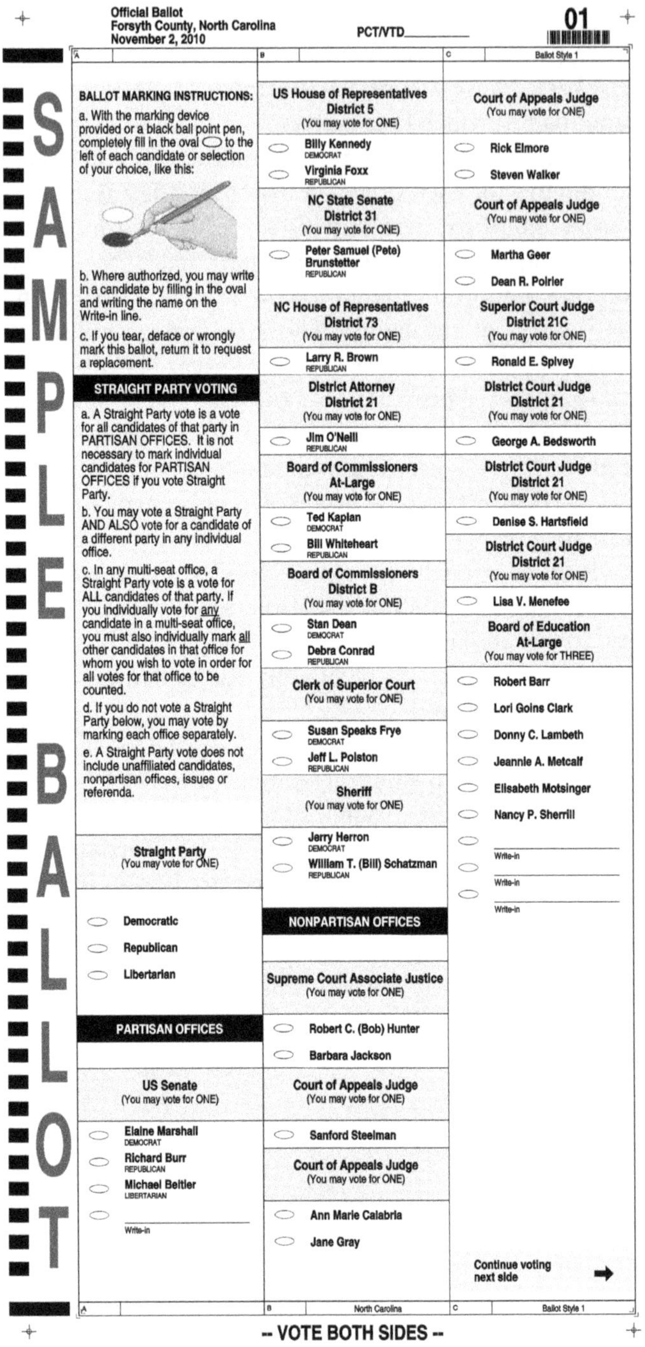

How the Ballot "Nudges" Voters

Official Ballot
Forsyth County, North Carolina
November 2, 2010

PCT/VTD_____

01

Ballot Style 1

BALLOT MARKING INSTRUCTIONS:

a. With the marking device provided or a black ball point pen, completely fill in the oval ⬭ to the left of each candidate or selection of your choice, like this:

b. Where authorized, you may write in a candidate by filling in the oval and writing the name on the Write-in line.

c. If you tear, deface or wrongly mark this ballot, return it to request a replacement.

STRAIGHT PARTY VOTING

a. A Straight Party vote is a vote for all candidates of that party in PARTISAN OFFICES. It is not necessary to mark individual candidates for PARTISAN OFFICES if you vote Straight Party.

b. You may vote a Straight Party AND ALSO vote for a candidate of a different party in any individual office.

c. In any multi-seat office, a Straight Party vote is a vote for ALL candidates of that party. If you individually vote for any candidate in a multi-seat office, you must also individually mark all other candidates in that office for whom you wish to vote in order for all votes for that office to be counted.

d. If you do not vote a Straight Party below, you may vote by marking each office separately.

e. A Straight Party vote does not include unaffiliated candidates, nonpartisan offices, issues or referenda.

Straight Party
(You may vote for ONE)

○ Democratic
○ Republican
○ Libertarian

PARTISAN OFFICES

US Senate
(You may vote for ONE)

○ Elaine Marshall
   DEMOCRAT
○ Richard Burr
   REPUBLICAN
○ Michael Beitler
   LIBERTARIAN
○ _____
   Write-in

US House of Representatives
District 5
(You may vote for ONE)

○ Billy Kennedy
   DEMOCRAT
○ Virginia Foxx
   REPUBLICAN

NC State Senate
District 31
(You may vote for ONE)

○ Peter Samuel (Pete) Brunstetter
   REPUBLICAN

NC House of Representatives
District 73
(You may vote for ONE)

○ Larry R. Brown
   REPUBLICAN

District Attorney
District 21
(You may vote for ONE)

○ Jim O'Neill
   REPUBLICAN

Board of Commissioners
At-Large
(You may vote for ONE)

○ Ted Kaplan
   DEMOCRAT
○ Bill Whiteheart
   REPUBLICAN

Board of Commissioners
District B
(You may vote for ONE)

○ Stan Dean
   DEMOCRAT
○ Debra Conrad
   REPUBLICAN

Clerk of Superior Court
(You may vote for ONE)

○ Susan Speaks Frye
   DEMOCRAT
○ Jeff L. Polston
   REPUBLICAN

Sheriff
(You may vote for ONE)

○ Jerry Herron
   DEMOCRAT
○ William T. (Bill) Schatzman
   REPUBLICAN

NONPARTISAN OFFICES

Supreme Court Associate Justice
(You may vote for ONE)

○ Robert C. (Bob) Hunter
○ Barbara Jackson

Court of Appeals Judge
(You may vote for ONE)

○ Sanford Steelman

Court of Appeals Judge
(You may vote for ONE)

○ Ann Marie Calabria
○ Jane Gray

Court of Appeals Judge
(You may vote for ONE)

○ Rick Elmore
○ Steven Walker

Court of Appeals Judge
(You may vote for ONE)

○ Martha Geer
○ Dean R. Poirier

Superior Court Judge
District 21C
(You may vote for ONE)

○ Ronald E. Spivey

District Court Judge
District 21
(You may vote for ONE)

○ George A. Bedsworth

District Court Judge
District 21
(You may vote for ONE)

○ Denise S. Hartsfield

District Court Judge
District 21
(You may vote for ONE)

○ Lisa V. Menefee

Board of Education
At-Large
(You may vote for THREE)

○ Robert Barr
○ Lori Goins Clark
○ Donny C. Lambeth
○ Jeannie A. Metcalf
○ Elisabeth Motsinger
○ Nancy P. Sherrill
○ _____ Write-in
○ _____ Write-in
○ _____ Write-in

Continue voting next side ➡

North Carolina   Ballot Style 1

-- VOTE BOTH SIDES --

FIGURE 2.4 Ballot with party box

2.3 Nudging Voters

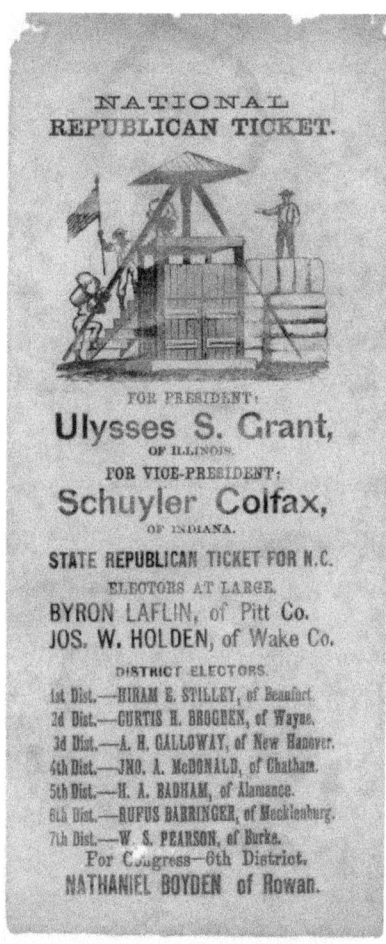

FIGURE 2.5 Party ballot, North Carolina, 1868

Scan of original from the North Carolina Collection at the University of North Carolina's Wilson Library.

of all parties on the ballot it became much easier to cast a split ballot (Rusk 1970).

However, we contend that the design of the Australian ballot also affects the propensity of voters to cast a split-ticket ballot. A ballot design that lines candidates into party columns encourages straight-ticket voting. For voters looking to make quick decisions, the party column facilitates an easy series of choices. One only need go down a column making a series of marks. The addition of a straight-ticket option on the ballot further encourages straight-ticket voting. It is a cognitively cheap and physically easy way for a voter to make voting decisions. In contrast, we contend that the office bloc ballot promotes greater cross-party voting by focusing the voter's attention on each race individually. Voters, of course, can and do cast a straight ticket with an office bloc ballot, but this design focuses more attention on the names of the candidates than the candidate's party affiliation. Rabid partisans are likely unaffected by ballot design, but past research has found that the impact of ballot design on split ticket voting is substantial for independents and weak party identifiers (Campbell and Miller 1957). It is these types of voters who are more likely to be nudged by the structure of the ballot placed in front of them.

From the perspective of strategic ballot architects, these effects provide strong incentives to choose ballot formats depending on external electoral conditions. Politicians wishing to insulate themselves from unfavorable national tides or an unpopular candidate at the head of the ticket should prefer the office bloc without a straight-ticket option. By forcing voters to make candidate-by-candidate choices and downplaying party labels, down ballot candidates can more easily carve out local electoral niches. Conversely, down ballot politicians wishing to link themselves with favorable national tides or a popular top of the ticket candidate should prefer the party column ballot and/or the straight-ticket option.

2.3.2 Completing the Ballot

In addition to split-ticket voting, ballot formats can nudge the propensity of voters to complete their ballot or leave some offices blank – also known as ballot roll-off. The office bloc ballot has been shown to increase ballot roll-off (e.g., Walker 1966). The necessity of making office-by-office choices leads some voters to give up after a while and fail to complete voting for all offices. This fatiguing effect of the office bloc ballot is especially pronounced among less educated and less partisan voters (Walker 1966). These voters tend to be less well informed about many of the choices on the ballot and hence are much more likely to not vote in these races, inducing ballot roll-off. In contrast, the party column ballot organizes the ballot by party and thus encourages voters to weight party identification more heavily in their decision calculus, thus producing less ballot roll-off. Moreover, one would suspect that the presence of a straight-ticket provision will reduce roll-off. By making a single mark, a voter can complete their ballot with one efficient decision.

From the perspective of strategic ballot architects, the choice of whether to include the party box can have considerable down ballot effects. Depending on the partisan composition of the electorate, down ballot candidates may desire to engineer roll-off or increase participation among those voting blocs who are less committed voters.

2.3.3 Waiting to Vote

The structure of the ballot has an influence not just in the voting booth but also outside the polling place. The absence of a straight-ticket option increases the amount of time and physical effort to complete the ballot. The increased time needed to complete the ballot can then lead to long lines at polling places. Long lines have been shown to discourage voters from voting, increase economic costs for those who wait in long lines, and reduce voter confidence in elections. A field study of voters in California, for example, found that having more than five people in a voting line tripled the probability of a prospective voter turning around and going home (Spencer and Markovits 2010).

Moreover, long lines at polling places are not uniformly distributed. Long lines tend to be found in urban areas and places with large minority populations. For example, the average waiting time for African-American voters in 2012 was 23.3 minutes compared to 11.6 minutes for white voters (Stewart, III 2015).

The implications of these results for ballot architects is clear. Those wanting to increase lines, and demobilize segments of the electorate, will opt for the office bloc ballot or the removal of a straight-ticket option. Either might lead to increased waiting times at polling places and serve to discourage turnout. Republicans in North Carolina, for instance, combined the elimination of the straight-ticket provision with a reduction in the number of days and hours available for early voting. The potential impact of both these changes fell heavily on African Americans and college students. Both groups also happen to be among the staunchest bloc of Democratic voters.

2.4 IMPLICATIONS FOR CANDIDATES

In a similar vein, as we show in Chapter 4, ballot architecture can also nudge the propensity of voters to support incumbent candidates. One of the long-standing findings in the literature on American elections, and congressional elections in particular, is that incumbents generally enjoy a substantial electoral advantage over their challengers. The size and scope of the incumbency advantage have certainly varied over time but the general finding is that incumbents have historically benefited from running as an incumbent. A vast literature has probed the sources of this advantage. Indeed, one can frame the last forty years of scholarship on congressional elections as a quest to find the sources of the incumbency advantage.

We present evidence in this book that ballot architecture can significantly influence the incumbency advantage. Members running for reelection on an office bloc ballot perform significantly better against challengers than do incumbents running on a party column ballot, all else equal. The office bloc design, we find, nudges voters to make more deliberate decisions, on the margin, for each office. As a result they are more likely to weigh the characteristics of candidates in each separate race that may boost the advantages of incumbents. The party column, by contrast, will nudge some voters toward voting a straight ticket. For voters casting a simple straight-party ticket, the impact of incumbency should matter less in their decision-making. This nudge effect will downweight the importance of incumbency for some voters and thereby reduce the electoral advantage of incumbency. At the same time, voters may end up voting for someone they would not have chosen if they had been more fully informed.

Careerist incumbents, we suspect, would prefer the office bloc ballot, all else equal. But of course these politicians are also members of party teams. What is in the collective interest might differ from the interests of individual candidates. We will see that this tension between the individual incentives of politicians and the collective incentives of parties occasionally conflicted in interesting and important ways.

2.5 BALLOT ARCHITECTURE OVER TIME

Throughout the nineteenth century the chief architects of the ballot were state and local political parties. When voters went to the polls on election day, they were given party ballots that were printed and distributed by the parties themselves rather than by a government agency. Each party designed its own ballot, often in a distinctive size and color, to ensure that individuals were voting for the party's slate of candidates. Moreover, voting was not a private act. Voters typically cast their ballots in public.

Any interested observer, including party workers, could watch and note how a voter cast their ballot.

In 1888, Massachusetts became the first American state to adopt a statewide Australian ballot (Ware 2002). Instead of being printed by parties the reformed ballot was printed and distributed by state and local governments. In doing so the new ballot consolidated all races and candidates onto a single ballot. Moreover, provisions were typically made for increased secrecy of voting. Following the lead of Massachusetts, many other states quickly adopted the Australian ballot so that by 1900, most states had moved to some variant of the Australian ballot.

To explore how ballot architecture has shaped American elections over the last century, we have compiled a dataset of state ballot laws from 1888 through 2008. While data on the period between 1888 and 1940 has been readily available for decades, data on state ballot laws in the post–World War II era proved more difficult to collect. In the pre-war era, many secondary sources contain these data such as Albright (1942) and Ludington (1911). In the post-war era, we were able to find data through the early 1950s from various issues of the Book of the States, but from approximately 1955 onward there are apparently no secondary sources that contain data on ballot laws. For the period after 1955, we relied on state statute books, historical newspapers, and interviews with selected Secretary of State offices.

This data collection effort has resulted in a comprehensive dataset on ballot structure in American elections over the last 130 years. It is worthwhile at the outset to simply document some of the more interesting features of the data. Figure 2.6 presents over-time trends in the distribution of party column and office bloc ballots. The first thing to note is that for most of the period from the initial adoption of ballot reform (in the 1890s) to the mid-1960s the majority of states opted for the party column format. Interestingly, however, the trend more recently has been toward the office bloc ballot. This trend became even more pronounced beginning in the early 2000s. We suspect it was the product of the Help America Vote Act and the increasing use of electronic voting machines. We will have more to say about these more recent changes in Chapter 5. Moreover, as noted in the introduction, since the 2000 election, a number of states have removed the straight-ticket option from the ballot.

The aggregate data mask, to some degree, the extent of changes over time. Thus it is also interesting to look at the frequency of ballot changes. Confining the analysis to just major changes in format from office bloc to party column or vice versa – there have been more than eighty total

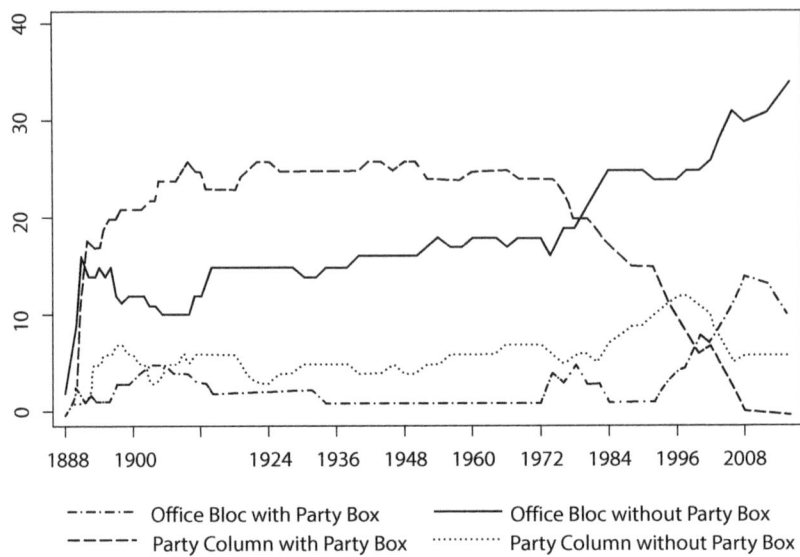

FIGURE 2.6 Ballot type by State, 1888–2008

changes. The biggest cluster of changes came in the early years after the first adoption of the Australian ballot. Between 1888 and 1950 there were twenty-eight changes. Most of those happened before 1930.

In the early part of the twentieth century, state and local candidates were more likely to have their success tied to the success of presidential candidates (Engstrom and Kernell 2014). For local parties hoping to capitalize on favorable national tides, a party column ballot with a straight party ticket provision offered a tantalizing opportunity.

In other places, state and local politicians found themselves at cross-purposes from national candidates such as presidential nominees. Running the agrarian populist William Jennings Bryan at the top of the Democratic ticket caused havoc for many eastern, urban Democratic candidates. For local politicians in these situations, an office bloc ballot without a straight ticket might nudge some voters toward splitting their ticket. Thereby ballot design could provide some institutional insulation for down ballot candidates against a locally unpopular national nominee.

Inter-party struggles were also correlated with race in parts of the country. Border states, like Maryland, had significant African-American populations. In the aftermath of the Civil War and Reconstruction, African Americans were strong supporters of the Republican Party. A ballot nudge that made it easier for African Americans to vote a straight ticket, such as the party column combined with party emblems, was thereby favored by the Republicans. Democrats, on the other hand found, it in their interest to choose an architecture that made it more difficult for pro-Republican African Americans to vote a straight ticket. The politics of ballot laws in early twentieth century Maryland, for example, offers a striking example of the back-and-forth driving ballot law changes.

In addition to inter-party struggles, there was also intra-party competition between reformers and party regulars, as we will see in Chapter 3's case study of Progressive-era California. Both parties had reform elements. Progressive Republicans, like Hiram Johnson in California, took direct aim at the old party machines. Johnson, for example, championed the use of the pure office bloc ballot as a way to reduce the influence of the party regulars. The Republican Party regulars with close ties to the Southern Pacific Railroad pushed hard for the party column ballot. The party column reduced uncertainty and nudged voters away from acting independently in their vote. Such intra-party struggles could be found in other parts of the country as well. In New York state, the fierce struggle between Tammany Hall Democrats and reform-oriented politicians played out in the fights over the format of ballot laws (Reynolds and McCormick 1986).

From 1950 until the end of the twentieth century, the frequency of ballot changes dropped. From 1950 to 2000, there were twenty-two changes. In the middle of the twentieth century, the level of competition between the parties receded. The political aftermath of the Great Depression, and the election of 1932, reduced party competition in many parts of the country. From 1932 until 1980, the Democratic Party held a solid lock on Congress, with the brief exceptions of the 1952 and 1956 elections. The muted competition for control of the national government led to an electoral era dominated by incumbents of both parties (e.g., Cain et al. 1987; Carson et al. 2007; Erikson 1971). Here the strategic problem of politicians was less on inter-party competition, as the value of marginals seats declined, but on protecting incumbents from adverse political winds. The incentives to tinker with ballot architecture followed suit.

More recently, the period from 2000 until the present has seen a substantial uptick in changes to ballot formats. Between 2000 and 2008, there were twenty overall changes in ballot formats, almost all toward the office bloc ballot. One explanation for the large number of changes in the 2000s is the passage of the Help America Vote Act. The difficulty of fitting a party column ballot onto a computer screen may have prompted states to switch to the office bloc. But a second, complementary, explanation concerns the altered partisan environment. As we will see in the study of North Carolina and Michigan in Chapter 5, the resurgence of nationalized parties and party polarization has reaccelerated the use of ballot formats for political gain.

The rekindled interest by politicians to use ballot laws for gain can clearly be seen in the recent trend to remove the straight-ticket provision. Since the late 2000s a substantial number of states have removed the straight-ticket option from the ballot. The general trend against the straight-ticket option has resulted in a quiet partisan revolution to America's electoral structure. This is explored more fully in Chapter 5.

2.6 ARE BALLOT ARCHITECTS AWARE?

A key premise of our study is that ballot architects understand the impact of ballot design and make strategic decisions about their preferred choice of format. But the question arises: Are these choice architects actually aware of their potential impact? For instance, the local election administrators in Palm Beach County were, by all accounts, not fully cognizant of the consequences of the butterfly ballot. And they certainly could not have anticipated that a seemingly mundane design decision would essentially decide who would assume the American presidency.

We will present considerable evidence throughout this book showing that most of the time ballot architects know what they are doing and act strategically in deciding what format to advocate. This is especially true when it comes to the decisions made in state legislatures regarding the structure and format of election ballots.

Two examples illustrate the point. The first is from the late nineteenth century (and discussed in more detail in Chapter 3). While fighting over ballot reform New York politicians expressed conscious concerns over how differing ballot architectures might nudge individual choices and aggregate together into favorable election outcomes. After hearing about recent elections in Massachusetts, the Democratic Governor of New York, David Bennet Hill, was alarmed by the potential partisan consequences of choosing an office bloc ballot. According to Fredman (1968, 45), Hill received "alarming news" from a friend in Massachusetts: "There was no provision for illiterates and the office block arrangement had encouraged splitting of the ticket and neglect of lower offices." The correspondent went on to write that the bulk of split-ticket votes went against Democrats. Realizing the politically dangerous consequences Hill went on to veto a number of attempts by the legislature to pass ballot reform.

The second example comes from the recent attempt by Republicans in Michigan to remove the straight-ticket provision from the Michigan ballot (discussed more fully in Chapter 5). The Michigan legislature voted to remove the straight-ticket provision in 2015. The passage of the law was on a close party line vote with Republicans promoting the removal while Democrats opposed the change. The roll-call pattern is itself very suggestive that partisan motives were behind the decision to remove the straight ticket. But evidence revealed during subsequent legal proceedings erased any doubt that Republican leaders were using the ballot law for partisan gain. They clearly knew exactly what they were doing. Lobbying efforts to change the ballot in Michigan were intense. They were led by the Michigan Republican Party Chairwoman, future chair of the Republican National Committee (Ronna Romney McDaniel), and cheered on by the future Secretary of Education, Betsy DeVos. Text conversations, revealed during the discovery process, show calculated partisan intent behind the push for removal of the straight-ticket option.

As we will see, these are just two of a number of examples we provide throughout the book. Aside from the obvious partisan implication of these choices we think the ballot design issue highlights important normative issues with regards to the trade-offs involved in designing democracy. More efficient ballot design, we will show, leads to higher participation rates and lower rates of ballot roll-off. Normatively, this is a very inclusive design that may encourage voters to make decisions in electoral contests that they have given little or no consideration to. In the early twentieth century, literacy rates were lower and waves of new immigrants may not have understood English well. Voting architecture that made it easier for these voters – such as party emblems on ballots – promoted a more inclusive electorate. In recent elections, the straight-ticket provision makes it easier to efficiently vote and reduces the waiting lines at polling places. To the extent we want to encourage an inclusive electorate, certain types of ballot designs help foster that goal.

Conversely, some critics of ballot features such as the straight-ticket option say that it makes it too easy for voters to cast votes for candidates and positions that the voters have not consciously decided to vote for. Some voters may have made a choice for the top of the ticket that fully determines their vote all the way down the ballot. Making the voter process less efficient and less inclusive will, as we show, reduce ballot completion rates in down ballot races. Whether these provisions weed out only those who are not making a conscious choice in these races is not something we can assess with our data.

A second trade-off concerns who should be designing the rules of the game. Currently, politicians design the balloting systems that can and do affect how voters use the tools of democracy to hold them accountable. The conflict of interest in such a system is apparent to anyone who has given this issue even cursory attention. Politicians are very clearly incentivized to design the electoral system in such a way to promote their own self-interest. An advantage is that these politicians are accountable to voters, but the sheer act of making choices about ballot design can insulate politicians from the ramifications of their decisions. A nationalized and stable set of ballot design rules would insure that all voters experience democracy similarly, but would also inhibit the ability of local officials to make design choices that better fit the customs and practices of their localities.

Finally, as is true of many issues in American politics, the recent efforts by many state legislatures to make the act of voting more difficult has clear interactions with racial politics in these states. Given the long history of racially discriminatory voting laws in the US, many argue that these laws are intended to suppress the voting rights of African-Americans. At the same time, African Americans, as a bloc, are one of the most reliable voting groups in the Democratic Party. As such, many critics of more inclusive voting policies claim that these policies are simply thinly veiled attempts to boost the electoral fortunes of the Democratic Party. As these examples illustrate, ballot design encompasses issues that go far beyond the obvious clerical and administrative tasks involve – it involves fundamental questions of fairness, equality, and partisan politics. It is against this backdrop that we frame our analyses of ballot design decisions and consequences. We begin to empirically examine these and other issues in Chapter 3 on the Progressive Era of ballot reform in the US.

3

Ballot Architecture in the Progressive Era

3.1 INTRODUCTION

The previous chapter introduced the idea that ballot architecture serves as an institutional solution to strategic problems faced by party politicians. As the problems faced by parties change over time so do the incentives to manipulate electoral architecture. This chapter and the next two demonstrate how the interaction between electoral problems and the choice of ballot architecture has shaped elections and representation over the past 140 years.

In this chapter we focus on the causes and consequences of ballot law architecture in the period between 1880 and 1940. We argue that two specific strategic problems drove ballot design decisions in this era. The first were considerations of how the ballot format would channel national electoral forces into state politics. In some states, parties employed the party column hoping to preserve a strong degree of straight-ticket voting. The office bloc format, on the other hand, weakened the linkage between presidential and lower-level candidates. Parties looking to shield themselves from national forces were more likely to prefer this format.

The second driver of choices over ballot formats was the cleavage between reform politicians versus old-guard party regulars. In this battle, each side turned to ballot laws as an institutional solution to their strategic problems. The party machines were aiming to hold onto power in an era of widespread economic, social, and political reform. The machines adapted to the secret ballot era by trying to craft ballot architecture that would ensure straight-ticket voting and minimize uncertainty on election day (Ware 2002). By contrast, progressive reformers sought to fashion ballot laws that would loosen the grip of party machines over voters. Reformers favored ballot formats that promoted independence — such as the pure office bloc ballot.

We start this chapter with a brief overview of the managerial difficulties that first led state parties to adopt the secret ballot at the turn of the twentieth century. We then examine the politics behind specific ballot design choices, with detailed attention given to California, New York, and Maryland. We show in these cases that parties were wrestling with the question of how to adapt their electoral strategies to both a competitive electoral environment and to the mounting calls from reform groups to clean up electoral politics. Ballot architecture became an institutional tool party politicians used to manage the dilemmas caused by these changing strategic circumstances. We conclude the chapter by showing how these alterations in ballot formats fundamentally shaped turnout, ballot roll-off, and the responsiveness of elections.

3.2 FROM PARTY BALLOTS TO SECRET BALLOTS

The widespread adoption of secret ballot laws between 1888 and 1920 is perhaps the single most important historical transformation in American electoral architecture. Prior to the implementation of the state-printed secret ballot, political parties were responsible for designing and printing election ballots. When voters went to the polls on election day, they were given party ballots that were printed and distributed by the parties rather than by the government. Only candidates of a single party were listed on these ballots – see Figure 2.5. Each party designed its own ballot, often in a distinctive size and color or even smell. In effect, the party ballot ensured that voters cast their vote for a party's entire slate of candidates as to cast a split-ticket the voter would have to physically change the names on the ballot. Moreover, voting during this era was not a private act as it was clear to observers which ballot a voter chose and the ballot box itself was often in open view.[1]

Starting in the late 1880s, and continuing through the next two decades, states across the nation began passing legislation that replaced the party ballot system with a state-printed secret ballot. Commonly known as the Australian ballot, named after the country of its origin, this reform had numerous key provisions that distinguished it from the

---

[1] George Caleb Bingham's "County Election" prevents a vivid portrait of voting in this era. See www.slam.org/countyelection/ for more information.

party ballot. First, balloting was to be conducted in secret, often behind a curtain. Second, the printing and distribution of ballots would be done by state and local governments, not the individual parties and their workers. Finally, there would only be a single consolidated ballot, listing candidates of all eligible parties for each office being contested. The first Australian ballot law was passed in 1888 in Kentucky, although its application was limited to Louisville. Later that year Massachusetts passed a statewide Australian ballot law. Reform spread rapidly after that.

By the end of 1891, thirty-three states had adopted the Australian ballot, and by 1912 all but two states had an Australian ballot. The relatively quick, and widespread, adoption of ballot reform has long puzzled historians and political scientists. Why would the strong parties of the Gilded Age pass such a seemingly self-defeating reform? The past literature points to a number of mutually compatible explanations.

One impetus for reform was growing public displeasure with corruption at the ballot box. Stories of vote purchasing were rampant throughout the 1880s (Summers 2004). During the 1888 presidential election, charges that both parties openly purchased votes in Indiana and transported out-of-state voters into New York filled newspapers throughout the country (Summers 2004; Walsh 1987).

Dissatisfaction with election fraud, and corruption in government more generally, spurred the formation of reform groups throughout the nation. In Massachusetts, for instance, the promotion of ballot reform was almost single-handedly led by the Mugwump Richard Henry Dana III. Perhaps nothing drew the ire of these good-government reformers more than vote buying. By the late 1880s, party leaders had reduced vote buying to an exact science. In Indiana, for example, "undecided" voters were grouped into blocks of five and assigned a party worker whose sole job was to hand out cash and monitor their designated "block of five." According to reformers, public voting and party-supplied ballots were the institutional linchpins of unchecked vote buying.

Thus, a good portion of the initial impetus for the Australian ballot came from reform groups seeking to eliminate corruption and vote buying at the polls. Central to the reform were provisions for secrecy. Party agents, the argument went, would be unwilling to pay for votes they could not guarantee would be delivered (Cox and Kousser 1981). Moreover, there would only be a single ballot, listing candidates of both parties. The public provision of a consolidated ballot was intended to stop intimidation by ticket peddlers and promote independence among voters.

While reformers had ample reason to push for secret ballot laws, it is less clear why the major parties did not do more to stop reform. The most compelling answer to this question is that ballot reform offered parties an institutional solution to a number of managerial problems they faced at the end of the nineteenth century. One aspect of the political environment at the end of the nineteenth century was the increasing urbanization of the country. In the context of party politics a rural, face-to-face society made it easier to mobilize and turn out voters (Cox and Kousser 1981). For party leaders, the challenges of managing both candidates and voters, and hence winning elections, greatly increased in urban centers as their populations increased.

In 1840, only 11 percent of the population lived in areas defined by the US Census Bureau as urban. By 1900, nearly 40 percent of the populace lived in urban areas. To be sure, there was significant geographic variation in where urbanization took place. And the majority of the country remained rural. But the growth of the cities, coupled with rapid immigration, substantially raised the challenges of managing hierarchical party organizations. As such, parties could no longer be sure they were getting their ballots into the hands of the proper voters. Voters, some of whom were illiterate or for whom English was not their native language, could not be sure they were voting with the proper ballot given the ease of producing fraudulent ballots.

Additionally, local renegade factions or candidates would often use the decentralized process of printing ballots to extort concessions from the state or national party organizations. If the local factions were not bought off, they might engage in ballot sabotage. This took various forms including not placing the proper candidates on the ballot, "knifing" through certain names on the ballot, and encouraging the use of pasters (see Figure 3.1) that allowed the name of a party nominee to be covered up with a different name (Reynolds and McCormick 1986, 43).

In short, shifting population demographics created large information asymmetries between state party officials and their local subordinates. As a result, state party bosses could not be sure if their local subordinates were printing and distributing the proper ballot. Without an effective monitoring system, parties suffered increased agency loss as they tried to corral their various local factions and voters. Parties experimented with oil-based ballots to prevent the use of pasters, but that did not prevent other forms of treachery, such as simply printing the wrong name on the ballot. The result of all this might be multiple tickets at the ballot box, wreaking havoc on the regular organization's electoral slate.

3.2 From Party Ballots to Secret Ballots

FIGURE 3.1 Example of a ballot poster

Note: Scan of original from the John H. Bryan papers in the North Carolina Collection at the University of North Carolina's Wilson Library. We thank John Baughman for alerting us to this example.

In 1880, for instance, factional warfare almost sunk the Democrats in New York as Tammany Hall and Reform Democrats ran separate tickets for municipal offices. Moreover, the feud between the two factions opened the door to opportunistic Republicans looking to trade their local candidates in exchange for Democrats voting for Blaine at the top of the ticket. As a result of knifing and pasting, split-ticket voting increasingly became a problem for state parties, although it was located primarily at the lower end of the ticket. In fact, Reynolds and McCormick (1986) present town-level data from New York and New Jersey showing that split-ticket voting at the lower end of the ballot was quite common during the 1880s and 1890s.

The Australian ballot offered a solution to many of the aforementioned problems. Because it was printed and supplied by the state, access to the official ballot could be regulated and centralized by the party. Wayward factions and bolting candidates would have little option but to work through regular party channels if they wanted to have influence in the party. In fact, Reynolds and McCormick (1986) argue that "outlawing treachery" was precisely the reason behind the parties' eventual support of ballot reform in New Jersey and New York.

The major parties also saw an opportunity in using the new ballot to quell third-party movements. In the Dakotas, for example, Republicans sought to blunt the Populist movement by limiting third-party access to the ballot and prohibiting fusion between Democrats and Populists (Argersinger 1992). Adding to the difficulty for third parties and independent candidates, severe signature requirements or anti-fusion provisions could make gaining access to the ballot nearly impossible, thus forcing them back into the major party fold.

The combination of mounting public pressure, self-defeating factional fights, and upstart third parties induced Democratic and Republican politicians alike into supporting reform. In fact, the initial passage of ballot reform often garnered bipartisan support (Argersinger 1992; Wigmore 1889). For the major parties, the Australian ballot was appealing on a number of levels. With a state-printed ballot, a party organization could be sure that its preferred candidates would appear on the ballot with its label properly affixed to the candidates' names. This trademark control over the party label reduced the agency loss associated with factional treachery, as parties could be confident that the correct candidate names were on the ballot. The state-printed ballot also shifted the considerable cost of ballot printing from the party to the state and local government, hence freeing up party funds for other uses. Thus, parties chose to try to control the type of ballot architecture adopted rather than stand in the way of reform.

The delegation of ballot architecture to state governments did not reduce conflicts over design; rather, it just shifted the arena of conflict from the polling places to the state legislatures. The state legislatures were now responsible for writing and passing the statutes that proscribed the format and layout of election ballots.

As the historian Peter Argersinger (1992, 166), quoting one local politician, writes:

The law itself and its basic provisions for a secret, public ballot did not become the object of contention (except in rare cases as in New York) so much as the modifications of the Australian ballot system and the use that could be made of them did. As one opponent of subsequent ballot changes in South Dakota said, "The real trouble is the change from the law as it originally stood."

Indeed, alteration in ballot architecture was common in the early twentieth century (Ware 2002). Party column ballots were substituted for office bloc ballots and vice versa; straight-ticket provisions were added or removed; party emblems were added or removed; and in at least one instance a state – Missouri – reverted from the Australian ballot back to something akin to a party ballot.

As we noted in the introduction to this chapter, two strategic problems were at play in this period that drove ballot architecture decisions after the initial reform. The first was the role that a competitive national political environment played. Throughout much of this period, both parties had a reasonable shot at capturing control of national institutions. The relatively strong role that national electoral forces played compelled some state parties to prefer the party column, while other state parties preferred the office bloc ballot. What was critical was whether or not the state party in power was aligned with the favorable national electoral tides.

The second factor influencing ballot formats was the differences between politicians aligned with party machines and those politicians who preferred to reform the electoral system. Reform politicians sought to fashion ballot laws that would loosen the grip of party machines over voters. A ballot architecture that promoted independence – such as the pure office bloc ballot – was often favored by reformers. The old-guard party politicians, by contrast, preferred ballot formats that mimicked the consolidated party ballots of the mid-nineteenth century.

In the rest of this chapter, we examine how these conflicting strategic imperatives drove ballot architecture decisions between 1880 and 1940. We first consider in detail the cases of California, Maryland, and New York. These states provide important illustrations of the two major political considerations that drove the design ballot architecture – the architecture of which is still largely in place today in these states. We then turn to a broader statistical analysis of ballot choice across all the states between 1888 and 1940.

3.3 CALIFORNIA

California first adopted the Australian ballot in 1891, opting for an office bloc format. The state modified its format a number of times over the next twenty years. California's politicians regularly fought over ballot structure even before the adoption of the Australian ballot. The combination of intra-party factions and intense inter-party competition led to frequent manipulation of the ballot format.

The passage of a secret ballot law, in 1891, featured a pitched political battle in the legislature. The fight was less over whether to pass a secret ballot law and more over the format that ballot would take. To get a bill passed, the party regulars successfully amended the bill by adding a straight-ticket voting provision, or what they called a party circle. This was a circle above each party's column allowing voters to cast a straight ticket with a single mark.

One of the strongest blocs in favor of the party circle format came from legislators connected to the Southern Pacific Railroad. The famed Political Bureau of the Southern Pacific held much influence in Sacramento, and across the state. The Political Bureau positioned a political manager in each county whose job it was to ensure the influence of the railroads in local and state elections (Hutchinson 1969). The intimate connection between the railroads and the legislature was perhaps nowhere more apparent than in US Senate elections. Notably, Leland Stanford was elected as a US Senator by the California legislature in 1885 while simultaneously serving as president of the Southern Pacific Company.

This is not to say that the railroad machine single-handedly ruled California politics. Some revisionist scholars have argued that the dominance of the Southern Pacific Company has been overstated (Williams 1973). But most scholars agree that the railroads, if not dominant, were certainly major players in the state's politics. The division between party regulars, backed by the railroads, and reformers formed a dominant cleavage line in California politics between 1870 and 1910.

Railroads were not the only significant economic player in California politics. At the local level, San Francisco barkeeps and saloon owners supplied financial backing for the party regulars. In exchange for favorable licensing from city councilmen, who partly owed their election to the work of the party regulars, the saloon businesses helped finance party operations. The party operatives then turned around and helped ensure the election of office-holders. The party regulars held up their end of the exchange by delivering votes on Election Day. Key to this exchange network was the ability of the regulars to reliably deliver votes.

A ballot structure that enhanced uncertainty about voter outcomes, like the secret ballot, made life more difficult for the party regulars.

They wanted confidence that a voter brought to the polls would be nudged to vote a consistent straight-party ticket. Thus, they preferred the party column with a straight-ticket voting provision. This reduced the unpredictable influence of the "independent voter" up and down the ballot.

As noted earlier, the format that emerged from the legislature was an office bloc format with a straight-ticket provision. Before the new ballot could take full effect, the California State Supreme Court tossed out the straight-ticket provision. The reasoning was that minor parties at the local level would not necessarily have candidates to head the top of the ticket. And therefore the straight-ticket provision discriminated against minor parties.

Between 1893 and 1898, divided partisan control of state government prevented any changes to ballot structure. The Republicans captured unified control of government in 1898 and in the ensuing session of the legislature (1899) passed a law switching the state to a party column ballot. The new law was pushed through by a Republican-dominated legislature hoping to reduce independent voting and nudge voters toward a straight, complete ticket. From the perspective of inter-party competition, the switch to a party column architecture made good political sense for the Republicans. The Republican congressional slate had run behind the presidential candidate in 1896, thus they stood to gain by switching to a more coattail-friendly ballot.

From the perspective of the struggle between party regulars and reformers within the Republican Party (also referred to as the GOP), the party column law acted as an attempt to maintain the influence of the regulars. As Petersen notes, it marked a temporary victory for the old guard Republican faction which, during the administration of Henry T. Gage, ruled the state according to dictates of the Southern Pacific's Political Bureau. Thus with a minimum of fanfare and publicity, the GOP-dominated legislature pushed through a bill aimed at reducing the difficulty in voting a straight-party ticket by arranging the names on the ballot in party columns (Petersen 1969, 125–126).

Both reform-oriented Republicans and Democrats cried foul. James H. Barry, publisher of the liberal San Francisco Star and lobbyist for the original bill, claimed the new law was a fraud, designed to hinder the voting of a split ticket (Petersen 1969, 126). Yet, with the legislature embroiled in the selection of a new US Senator, the new law passed without detailed press scrutiny.

The battle between reformers and the party regulars continued throughout the rest of the decade. Notably, the 1904 presidential victory of the Progressive Republican Theodore Roosevelt marked a turning point in the battle between reformers and the old-guard party regulars. The intra-party struggles of the California Republicans were a microcosm of these larger divisions within the national Republican Party. As these divisions played out in California, ballot architecture appeared to the party regulars as a means to insulate themselves from the growing tide of Progressivism. In his contemporaneous account of the 1911 California legislative session, the reporter Franklin Hichborn revealed how, earlier in the decade, the party column enabled the regular Republicans to ride the coattails of Theodore Roosevelt in the 1904 presidential election (Hichborn 1911, 88).

Roosevelt was highly popular statewide and carried California easily. But Roosevelt's commitment to reform conflicted with the aims of the regular Republicans of California who maintained a close association with the Southern Pacific political bureau. In this way, the party column with a party circle worked to stunt the efforts of reformers. Machine Republicans could survive on the party ticket even in the face of a national party that nominated a reform candidate at the top of the ticket. They became a thorn in the side of more Progressive Republicans in Congress.

Hichborn (1911, 89) writes:

Thus, under the "party circle" scheme of voting, the popularity of Roosevelt policies which gave Roosevelt his large California vote, at the same time carried the elections of representatives in Congress who were well calculated to act as a bloc in the way of realization of those policies. Roosevelt and a square deal was the rallying cry in California that year. Roosevelt carried the State, and at the same time pulled into office legislators who were for anything but square deal policies.

This ongoing dispute between reformers and party regulars culminated in the 1909 session, which saw the two sides battle across a number of policy fronts (Hichborn 1909, 1911). A number of pieces of reform legislation were attempted during the session. And one of the major conflicts in 1909 was an attempt by reformers to remove the party circle from the ballot. The vote to remove the party circle from the ballot failed in the Assembly by a single vote, with thirty-five yeas and thirty-six nays. The vote contains a number of interesting facets. First, all of the Democrats voted to remove the party circle. Given their small numbers in the legislature, this is not too surprising. Removing the party circle would have made it easier for down-ballot Democrats to detach themselves from the unpopular top of the ticket. The Republicans had carried the state in the last four presidential elections and had won the 1904 and 1908 statewide vote by healthy margins.

Second, and perhaps even more interesting, were the votes of the Republicans. Seventeen voted for removing the party circle and thirty-six voted to maintain the status quo. All of the votes to maintain the party circle came from these Republicans. The next question is whether the Republicans supporting the party circle were part of the regular Republican faction. Fortunately, the session provided a number of other votes related to political and economic reform.

In particular, the legislature voted on a motion calling for a line of government-owned steamships. The steamships were to run from San Francisco to Panama. In other words, they posed a direct threat to the railroad's dominance of shipping. The vote in the Assembly concerned bringing the bill from committee to the floor. The vote provides a strong indicator of a legislator's support or opposition to railroad regulation. A no vote was a pro-railroad vote while a yes vote represented the reform side (Hichborn 1909).

Fully 85 percent of those voting to remove the party circle also voted in favor of the railroads. The percentages are even higher for just Republicans. Among Republicans 93 percent of those who supported removing the party circle also supported the position of the railroads (Hichborn 1909). In short, these numbers reveal the tight linkage between support for the railroads and maintaining the straight-ticket provision of the ballot.

The state finally settled on a pure office bloc ballot in 1911. The 1911 legislation followed the pivotal 1910 election. This election witnessed the successful progressive campaign of Hiram Johnson for governor and the election of a large bloc of progressives to the state legislature. Johnson had campaigned on a vigorous platform of progressive reform, which included a call for returning to the office bloc ballot (or the original ballot as he called it). Indeed, he included the passage of an office bloc bill in his 1911 inaugural address. The new legislature passed the office bloc ballot by a unanimous vote in both chambers. Even those state senators who had opposed reform in the previous sessions, following the strong Progressive winds, now voted for the office bloc.

Beyond the revealing political dynamics over ballot architecture, California also presents an important test case of the impact of ballot laws.

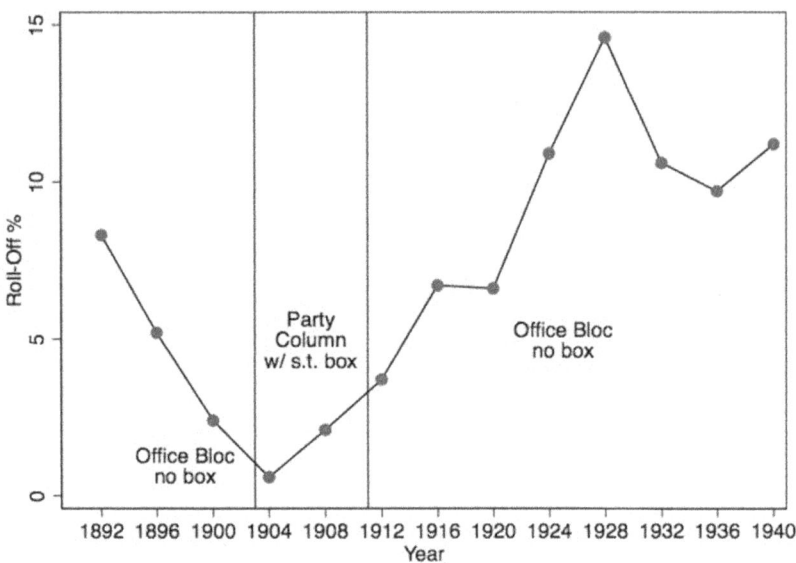

FIGURE 3.2 Roll-off by ballot type, California

It was one of the few states to bounce back and forth between the two ballot formats. The impact of different ballot formats on roll-off can be seen in Figure 3.2. Ballot roll-off between presidential and congressional elections was negligible in the years before the Australian ballot. Roll-off sharply increased following the initial passage of ballot reform in its office bloc format. The switch to the party column format, in 1899, shrunk ballot roll-off bringing it back to low levels. And finally, the restoration of an office bloc ballot in 1911 led to a large uptick in roll-off.

3.4 NEW YORK

The initial adoption of the Australian ballot generated bi-partisan support in most states. In New York, however, reform was a decidedly partisan affair. Republicans in the state legislature pushed for ballot reform. But the legislation was repeatedly vetoed by the Democratic Governor David Bennet Hill. He vetoed an Australian ballot bill in 1888, 1889, and 1890. Finally, in 1890 the Republicans passed a version of reform but it was a very weak version of ballot reform. Each party had its own separate ballot, albeit printed by the state. Republicans in the state legislature attempted again in 1894 to pass a stronger version of ballot reform but this was again vetoed by the Democratic governor. Following Republican victories in both state the state legislative and gubernatorial elections of 1894, the Republicans finally passed an Australian ballot bill. The new ballot consolidated all offices onto a single, state-printed ballot. This version of the ballot was organized in the party column format with a straight-ticket option – the most party-centered version of the Australian ballot.

The party column format remained in place until 1913 when the state switched to the office bloc format and removed the straight-ticket option. This time it was the Democratic Party leading the charge to change ballot formats. The Democrats had lost their majority in the lower chamber during the 1913 November state assembly elections. During a lame-duck session before turning power over to the Republicans, the Democrats passed a bill providing for an office bloc ballot.

Why were Democrats so interested in putting an office bloc ballot into place? Since 1892, no Democratic presidential candidate had received a majority in New York. Although the Democratic candidate, Woodrow Wilson, won the state in 1912, this was largely due to the split within the Republican Party. So, looking forward New York Democrats had good reason to suspect the presidential election would be problematic. A switch to the office bloc ballot offered the possibility of insulating down-ballot Democrats from these adverse national forces and allowing local candidates to emphasize their personal qualities.

Figure 3.3 displays the consequences. The figure shows roll-off percentages before and after the switch to the office bloc. Similar to the pattern we see below in Maryland, roll-off jumped sharply with the removal of the party column plus straight-ticket format. Roll-off from 1896 to 1912 averaged 1.98 percent. After the switch to the office bloc, roll-off more than doubled to an average of 4.18 percent (from 1916 through 1940).

3.5 MARYLAND

Maryland's initial Australian ballot law was passed in 1890 by a Democratic-controlled legislature, albeit with reluctance. The proponents of reform were a coalition of Republicans, Mugwumps, and independent Democrats. While the latter two groups were primarily interested in ridding the polls of corruption and vote buying, the

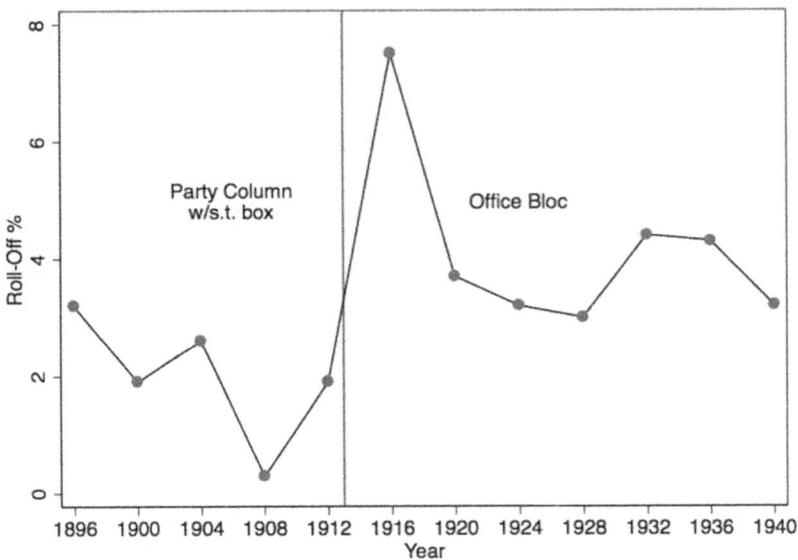

FIGURE 3.3 Roll-off by ballot type, New York

Republican motivation was to break the grip of the Democratic machine on state politics. Mounting public pressure for an Australian ballot law, and its successful deployment as campaign issue by the Republicans, convinced the Democratic organization to accede to reform in 1890 (Argersinger 1992).

Democrats did not completely cave in to all of the demands of the reform movement, however. In fact, the Democratic-dominated legislature clearly bent the new law in a pro-Democratic direction. Republicans had called for a "full Australian ballot" – by which they meant an office bloc layout without a straight-ticket option – but the Democrats instead opted for a party column format. One can see the partisan logic behind the Democrats' preference for the party column. Throughout the 1880s, their statewide and presidential ticket outpolled Republicans, but not by large margins. In this competitive environment, adopting a ballot format that might preserve the strong coattails of the old party strip ticket would help maintain Democratic majorities.

The Democrats reversed their position ten years later when, as part of a sweeping revision of the state electoral code, they switched the state to an office bloc format. The motivation, once again, had clear partisan overtones. The Democrats had recently regained control of the state legislature in 1900 after losing it in the pro-Republican landslide of 1896. Now back in power, the new Democratic majority publicly pledged a major overhaul of the state electoral rules. Central to these reforms was a vow to change the ballot layout by scrapping the party column format (Callcott 1986).

Lurking behind this change of heart was a not-so-hidden desire to disenfranchise poor whites and African-American voters. The new office bloc format eliminated the party emblems at the top of the ballot, making it difficult for illiterate voters to discern how to vote a straight ticket. Moreover, the new law required improperly marked ballots to be tossed out – a provision the was designed to have the largest impact on illiterate voters.[2] As the *New York Times* noted,

> Ex-Senator Arthur Pue Gorman and his friends are depending largely upon the intricacies of the new ballot at the coming election to secure their control of the Legislature, and assure his return to the United States Senate. They expect to disfranchise [sic], through mistakes and inability in the marking their ballots, a sufficient number of negro voters to enable them to carry the State.

The ballot change further worked to the electoral benefit of Democrats by weakening the connection between national and state candidates. Republicans carried the state in the two previous presidential elections (1896 and 1900) and Democrats further down the ballot had suffered immensely. This point was made evident during the 1900 campaign when the Democratic state boss Arthur Pue Gorman complained about having to conduct consecutive campaigns burdened with William Jennings Bryan at the head of the ticket. Gorman's complaints had a lot of merit. Maryland's US House delegation had completely flipped from a 6-0 Democratic advantage after the 1892 election to a 6-0 Republican advantage after the 1896 and 1900 elections.[3] Bryan's strident emphasis on the silver currency issue may have been popular in the agrarian Midwest, but it held little sway with voters in urban Baltimore. Gorman became so dissatisfied that he threatened to keep the Democratic organization out of the election altogether if Bryan were renominated. Gorman eventually relented, but Bryan's poor showing in the state, and his detrimental impact on down-ballot Democrats, prodded the Democrats to adopt a

---

[2] According to the 1910 US Census, 8.5 percent of voting-age males in Maryland were illiterate.

[3] Democrats recovered two seats in the midterms of 1898, but lost both again in 1900.

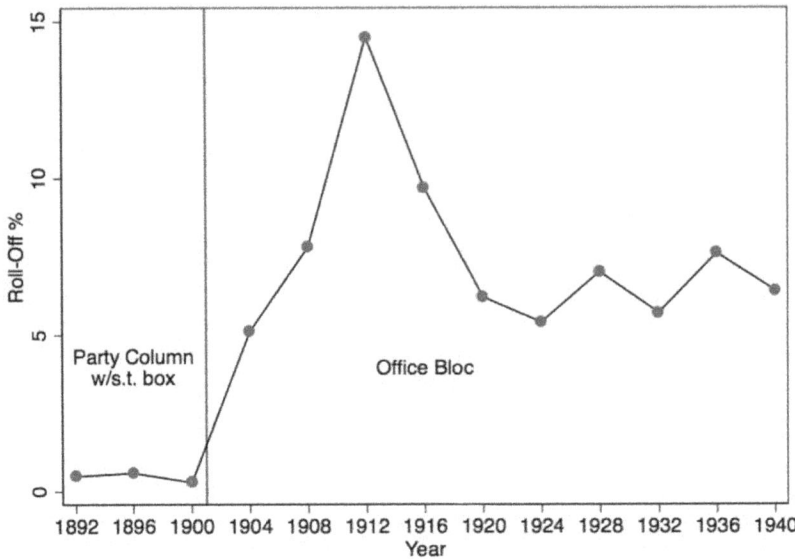

FIGURE 3.4 Roll-off by ballot type, Maryland

ballot format that would help detach the state ticket from burdensome presidential nominees.

Figure 3.4 reveals that switching to the office bloc had the effect of increasing ballot roll-off for congressional candidates. The figure displays the percentage difference between total votes cast for presidential candidates and total votes cast for US House candidates. As the figure shows, under the party column (with a straight-ticket box) roll-off was negligible. The average roll-off between 1892 and 1900 was a miniscule 0.47 percent. Roll-off jumped sharply, and immediately, upon the switch to a pure office bloc format. From 1904 through 1940 roll-off averaged 7.54 percent. This increased roll-off appears to have helped the Democrat's electoral fortunes. The statewide partisan vote remained highly competitive, but the Democrats continued to maintain comfortable majorities in the Maryland legislature, which controlled Senate appointments. In addition, the House delegation was split 3-3 after the 1904 and 1908 presidential elections, despite Bryan once again appearing at the top of the Democratic ticket in 1908.[4]

---

[4] Democrats lost an additional two seats by incredibly slim margins in 1908 – one district was lost by only 212 votes and a second by only 317. In both cases, votes for minor party candidates were greater than the difference between the Democrat and the Republican.

TABLE 3.1 *Partisan change in state ballot laws, 1888–1940*

	Non-Congruent	Congruent
Party Limiting	61.54	30.00
	(8)	(9)
Party Enhancing	38.46	70.00
	(5)	(21)

3.6 THE POLITICAL LOGIC OF BALLOT ARCHITECTURE

The three cases discussed earlier clearly demonstrate that the form of the ballot that voters encountered in these states had a substantial effect on observable political outcomes. We also see clear examples of strategic politicians manipulating the ballot form in order to maximize political gain or in some cases minimize potential losses. In this section, we provide a more comprehensive analysis of state ballot law changes from 1888 to 1940.

We begin by considering the political conditions under which states decide to make changes to the form of the ballot. As we discussed earlier, ballot features such as the party box and the party column ballot tend to encourage partisan voting and in doing so increase the symmetry of results from the top to the bottom of the ballot. Conversely, the office bloc ballot and the absence of a party box tends to delink the top from the bottom of the ticket and leads to an increase in ballot roll-off.

We coded each change in ballot form during this era as either being party enhancing (office bloc to party column, adding the party box) or a change in a party limiting direction (party column to office bloc, removal of party box). We also then coded each state's political environment as either congruent – same party wins at the presidential and state legislative level – or non-congruent – partisan divide between state and national winners. We would expect states with congruent political environments to adopt party enhancing changes such as we saw in California, while we expect states with non-congruent environments to adopt party limiting reforms, much like what we saw in the Maryland and New York cases.

The result of a cross-tabulation of these two variables is presented in Table 3.1. The results are clearly in line with our expectations. States with congruent political environments were more than twice as likely to adopt party enhancing rather than party limiting changes in the ballot form. Similarly, states with non-congruent political environments were

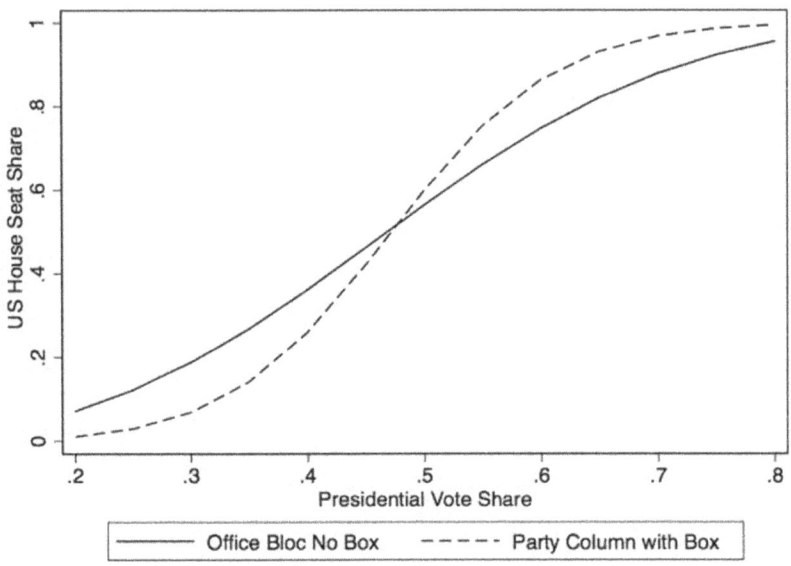

FIGURE 3.5 Seats/votes curve by ballot type, 1888–1940

much more likely to adopt party limiting changes in ballot forms. Overall, twenty-nine of the forty-three (67.4 percent) changes we observe are in the expected direction. A simple cross-tab such as that presented in Table 3.1 is not a definitive test of our expectations, but these results do suggest that the patterns we observed in our case studies are reflected in the larger data set of ballot forms changes.

The effects of ballot redesigns on outcomes provide clear evidence as to why strategic political actors regularly made changes to ballot form during this era. Figure 3.5 presents data on how the statewide presidential vote translated into seats in the US House by ballot type. In constructing the seats/votes curve, we compared the most party enhancing ballot form (party column with party box) to the least party enhancing form (office bloc without party box).

The results in Figure 3.5 demonstrate that the party column ballot with the party box is far more responsive than is the office bloc ballot without a box. These data suggest that the office bloc ballot's ability to insulate a party from national tides is consistent across this era.

What are the mechanisms behind these trends? As Rusk (1970) demonstrated, the office bloc ballot produces a higher incidence of

TABLE 3.2 *Effects of ballot type on roll-off and turnout, 1888–1940*

Variable	Coefficient (Std. Err.)	
	Roll-off	Turnout
Office Bloc No Box	2.53**	−6.60*
	(1.18)	(3.73)
Party Column No Box	1.40*	−2.82
	(0.78)	(3.15)
Office Bloc Box	0.83	−2.05
	(0.96)	(4.09)
Party Column Box	0.27	−3.19
	(0.69)	(3.12)
Presidential Competition	<0.01	−0.14***
	(0.01)	(0.03)
Year Counter	0.05*	−0.07
	(0.03)	(0.08)
Female Suffrage	−0.98	−10.22***
	(1.22)	(2.00)
Constant	−93.15*	220.34
	(54.24)	(158.09)
N	612	612
R^2	0.43	0.92

Note: Estimates are from a linear regression model. Standard errors clustered by state in parentheses. State and year fixed effects estimated but not reported. *** = $p \leq 0.01$; ** = $p \leq 0.05$; * = $p \leq 0.10$.

split-ticket voting than does the party column ballot. We also saw evidence from the case studies earlier that ballot roll-off increased significantly under the office bloc ballot.

3.7 IMPLICATIONS FOR BALLOT ROLL-OFF

In this section, we examine the impact of ballot architecture on roll-off more systematically. In each of the three case studies, we found a predictable pattern of ballot roll-off. The pure office bloc ballot increased roll-off considerably. By contrast, the party column, along with the straight-ticket provision, muted the degree of roll-off.

To systematically explore the consequences of ballot type on roll-off, we take advantage of the wide variation across, and within, states in ballot formats between 1888 and 1940. Specifically, we used a panel regression with both state and year fixed effects. The results of this difference-in-difference model are shown in the first column of Table 3.2. The dependent variable is voting roll-off between statewide presidential and congressional turnout. This is measured simply as the difference in turnout within a state among eligible voters for the president and the US House (Rusk 2001). The key independent variables are the format of the ballot. The four types of ballots included are: party column with a straight-ticket option, office bloc with a straight-ticket option, party column without a straight-ticket option, and office bloc without a straight-ticket option. The excluded, baseline, format is the party strip ballot that was present before Australian ballot reform. The model also includes a linear time trend to adjust for the possibility of an independent over time increase in ballot roll-off. The model also controls for statewide competition – measured as the difference in vote share between the Democratic and Republican presidential candidates – and a dummy variable denoting the year when a state provided for female suffrage.

The differential impact of ballot formats is shown in the first column of Table 3.2. The office bloc ballot without a straight-ticket option had the largest impact on roll-off. This format increased roll-off by 2.53 percent. But the party column minus a straight ticket also increased roll-off; under this format roll-off increased by 1.4 percent. The office bloc with a straight-ticket option increased roll-off by a small amount – 0.93 percent, but this difference was not statistically significant. The coefficient for the party column with a straight ticket was negligible and insignificant. The two most prominent ballot types were office bloc without a straight ticket (or pure office bloc) and party column with a straight ticket. Thus, the sharp differences between these two represent the most electorally consequential differences.

Given that congressional candidates typically appear near the top of the ballot, the numbers in the first column of Table 3.2 likely represent the lower bound of roll-off. Examining offices that appear further down the ballot (e.g., state legislators, attorney generals, lieutenant governors, etc.) would almost surely magnify the amount of roll-off when the straight-ticket option is absent. For down-ballot politicians, notably state legislators, wanting to insulate themselves from the top of the ticket, the office bloc must have looked quite attractive.

3.8 IMPLICATIONS FOR TURNOUT

As we noted earlier, under the old party strip ballot system, voters had little opportunity to register office-by-office choices. As a result, straight-ticket voting predominated. Moreover, voters typically deposited their party strip ballots in public. Any interested observers, such as party workers, could monitor voters as they cast these identifiable ballots (Bensel 2004). Party operatives could, therefore, be confident that a voter ushered to the polls, or given a payment, would dutifully vote for the entire party slate. As a result, the payoffs from mobilizing supporters, in terms of votes for multiple candidates of the same party, were considerable (Heckelman 1995).

The spread of the Australian secret ballot severely complicated the task of mobilizing voters (Engstrom 2012). Voters no longer had to worry about party operatives peering over their shoulder, but it also meant that party operatives could no longer directly ensure that those they polled (or paid) actually voted the way the party wanted. Moreover, by placing candidates of every party onto a single consolidated ballot, the new format eased the physical task of casting a split-ticket (Engstrom and Kernell 2014; Carson and Roberts 2013; Heckelman 1995; Rusk 1970). As a result, the incentives of elites to shepherd these less-reliable voters to the polls were severely diminished.

As we have seen, the physical format of the new Australian ballot – and hence its consequences – was not uniform. The two main ballot formats – office bloc or party column – had a clear, discernible impact on split-ticket voting. The office bloc ballot forced voters to manually work their way down the ballot and make separate choices for each office. The result was a significant uptick in split-ticket voting. In contrast, by emulating the old party strip ballots, the party column format still induced a substantial amount of straight-ticket voting (Rusk 1970). The consequences for mobilization decisions were substantial. Because the office bloc created more split-ticket voting, the rewards from mobilization diminished. Voters brought to the polls were now much less reliable as they were not sure to vote "properly" down ballot. On the other hand, ushering partisans to the polls in party column states remained a worthwhile investment.

The second column of Table 3.2 assesses the effect of ballot type on turnout. The model mirrors the one estimated for roll-off and the findings are somewhat similar. All four forms of the Australian ballot have a negative coefficient suggesting that they are associated with a decline in turnout. Of the four forms, the office bloc without party box has the largest coefficient and is the only estimate that reaches statistical significance. The effect, however, is quite large. The office bloc without box is associated with a 6.6 percent reduction in turnout, which is substantively quite large.

3.9 CONCLUSION

Taken as a whole, the results in this chapter emphasize a core theme of this book: The institutions governing ballot architecture are not exogenous to political competition. They can be altered by politicians in an attempt to solve short-term electoral problems. In this way, the rules of democracy are constructed through the process of party competition. This competition over the structure of American electoral institutions has profound effects on whether people vote and how they vote (Springer 2014).

In the specific case of the Progressive Era, we have illustrated the dramatic transformation in the nation's electoral system produced by the adoption of the Australian ballot. This resulted in much more heterogeneity nationally as states designed the voting process in ways that most suited their party's short-term political goals. This ranged from suppressing the vote in states like Maryland, to declines in responsiveness to national tides in states like New York. These differential voting systems produced considerable variance in responsiveness, ballot roll-off, and voter turnout. In Chapter 4, we show how the altered political landscape that started in the Progressive Era further transformed the incentives of ballot architects, leading to an electoral system that prized the personal characteristics of candidates at the expense of strong parties.

4

The Personal Vote Era, 1940–2000

4.1 INTRODUCTION

The political environment in the United States shifted in fundamental ways in the middle decades of the twentieth century. The hyper-partisan competition that had defined the late nineteenth century faded post–1896 and again during the New Deal era as Democrats were dominant in much of the country. With the Jim Crow regime firmly entrenched in the South there was little to no partisan political competition in that region (Aldrich and Griffin 2017). The Democratic dominance in the South helped tame battles for majority control of Congress as Democrats held majority control of the US House in all but two congresses between 1933 and 1995. Additionally, the advent of the direct primary took the power to control nominations for elective office from party elites and placed it in the hands of voters (Merriam and Overacker 1928). The combination of the 17th Amendment, the Australian ballot, and the direct primary cut many of the electoral ties binding parties and candidates together (Carson and Roberts 2013).

At the same time, Congress as an institution was evolving in ways that created incentives for members to seek long careers in the institution. After the revolt against Speaker Joseph Cannon in 1909, the decision-making structure of the House became more decentralized as power shifted from the party leadership to congressional committees (Schickler 2001). The seniority system also emerged during this time period (Katz and Sala 1996; MacKenzie 2015). The seniority system helped ensure that members who stayed in Congress for an extended period of time would accumulate power within the respective chambers regardless of their policy views. The concomitant rise of independent congressional committees and the seniority system served to empower committees generally and their leaders specifically (Polsby 1968). Writing about this so-called textbook era of the US Congress, Mayhew (1974, 27) wrote, "The fact is that no theoretical treatment of the United States Congress that posits parties as analytic units will go very far." The American Political Science Association was so struck by this state of affairs that they issued a now-infamous report calling for stronger and more cohesive parties.

Taken together these changes fundamentally altered both the dynamics of congressional elections and the internal dynamics of Congress. These changes empowered individual members of Congress, clarified their path to power, and made retention of seats in Congress more dependent on the actions and reputation of the incumbent and less dependent on the fate and actions of the member's party (Katz and Sala 1996). As a result, members began to pursue a "personal vote" in Congress (Cain et al. 1987; Carson et al. 2007) and the incumbency advantage in US House election increased dramatically (Cox and Katz 2002).

Not only did these institutional changes affect election dynamics, we argue they also altered the strategic problem facing ballot architects. Winning seats for one's party on the margin faded in importance and was replaced by the desire to extend political careers. As politicians became more careerist, they sought to shield themselves from adverse tides. The strategic design of ballot formats offered one solution to this problem. We argue in this chapter that this change in strategy helped drive the incumbency advantage in the US Congress as members adopted representational strategies that highlighted their personal accomplishments.

In some ways, the politics of ballot reform in this era were less fraught than they were during the two heavily partisan eras that bookend this era. As we will demonstrate below, there were few ballot laws changes that moved ballot laws in a partisan direction. As such, these changes tended to not be as controversial as they were in the era covered in Chapter 3.[1] A few cases, however, were quite compelling politically and as demonstrated later, the political *effects* of ballot reform during this time period were quite substantial even if the political drama was subdued.

---

[1] We spent a considerable amount of time trying to uncover the roll-call votes of many of these changes. In many cases, reforms during this were adopted by voice vote with minimal discussion or disagreement in the state legislature. As such, there is scant media coverage of many of the changes from this era.

We begin in the next three sections with an analysis of mid-twentieth century ballot architecture decisions in Ohio, Connecticut, and North Carolina. Each of these cases illustrates how state politicians used ballot architecture to protect careerist incumbents from adverse electoral tides. Not only were ballot architects responding to the changing electoral environment, they were also reinforcing that new electoral environment by choosing ballot formats that favored incumbent politicians.

4.2 OHIO: SAVING "MR. REPUBLICAN"

Ohio has been a political battleground for much of the nation's history. After the Civil War, for example, Ohio's elections often proved instrumental in deciding party control of national institutions. The razor-thin partisan division of the state electorate prompted Ohio politicians to continually tinker with institutional rules in the search for electoral victory. For instance, the state legislature redrew Ohio's US congressional districts six times between 1878 and 1892 (Engstrom 2013).

Ohio's importance in national elections continued into the twentieth century. The migration of African Americans from the South to the urban centers of the North, including Ohio, further altered the importance of Ohio to national politics. By the middle of the twentieth century, winning in Ohio was a crucial piece of the puzzle for capturing the presidency and control of Congress. For the Democratic Party, this meant being able to mobilize African American voters in Cleveland, Columbus, and Cincinnati. This political backdrop raised the stakes for Ohio's ballot architects in the middle of the twentieth century.

Ohio initially adopted the Australian ballot in 1891, settling on the party column with a straight-ticket option that is most akin to the old party ballot. This ballot type remained in place for more than fifty years. However, in November of 1949, a year-long campaign ended with Ohio citizens voting by more than 250,000 votes to amend the state's constitution, switching the ballot type from a party column to an office bloc ballot. The amendment also removed party symbols and the straight-party ticket from the Ohio ballot. Thus beginning with the 1950 election, Ohio switched from the ballot form most likely to produce party line voting – party column with a straight ticket option – to the form most likely to produce split-ticket voting – office bloc without a straight-ticket option.

What prompted Ohio's voters to make this change? The supporters of the amendment provide us a key clue. The campaign was explicitly led and supported by Ohio Republicans and, in particular, supporters of Senator Robert A. Taft also known throughout the country as "Mr. Republican." The push for ballot reform was, as it turns out, a direct response to Taft's performance in the 1944 election. Democrats had targeted Taft for defeat in 1944 and had in many ways pinned their hopes on the ballot structure. Taft's opponent, William Pickrel, was "uninspiring" to many in the Democratic coalition, but the party hoped that the combination of President Franklin D. Roosevelt and the gubernatorial nominee, Frank Lausche the popular Cleveland mayor, at the top of the ticket would boost Pickrel and that Taft would be "buried in the avalanche" (Patterson 1972, 273). The strategy almost worked. Taft barely survived the 1944 election, winning by only 17,000 votes out of more than three million cast.

According to Taft's biographer, he immediately pointed to the ballot as a reason for the closeness of the election, writing to a confidant that

The closeness of my election was due principally to Stewart's [Republican candidate for Governor] weakness, because, as you know, my name was about seventh on the state ballot and there was a tremendous amount of straight-ballot voting. ...With the Massachusetts ballot, [i.e. office bloc] I would have nearly broken even in Cleveland (Patterson 1972, 279).

Taft strongly encouraged the ballot reform movement and the clearly stated intent of the backers of ballot reform was to insulate Senator Taft from straight-ticket voting Democrats in urban areas. Of particular concern to Ohio Republicans and Taft supporters was his 1950 reelection campaign. Taft was again seeking reelection at the same time as popular Democratic Governor Frank J. Lausche.[2] Taft's supporters thought the ballot law change could net him at least 100,000 votes (Key 1952).

Going into the 1950 election, Taft had accumulated a great deal of power within the Senate. In fact, many labeled him the most powerful Republican senator in the country. He was the ranking minority member on the Labor and Public Welfare Committee and was the 2nd ranking Republican on the influential Senate Finance Committee. In terms of

---

[2] Lausche had a long and successful career in Ohio politics. He served as mayor of Cleveland from 1942–1944. He won election as governor in 1944, lost his reelection bid in 1946, and reclaimed the governor's office in 1948 by more than 221,000 votes, avenging the narrow 1946 loss. He would go on to serve as governor until 1957 before winning a seat in the US Senate where he served until 1969.

4.2 Ohio: Saving "Mr. Republican"

influence in the Senate, and projects supported by the federal government, it was reasonable to assume that the lives of Ohioans would change if someone other than Taft was elected in 1950.[3] In addition, Taft clearly had decided that he wanted to be the president. He had unsuccessfully sought the presidential nomination in both 1940 and 1948, thus a statewide rejection in Ohio would have likely have permanently ended his dream of becoming the president.[4] Taft's supporters spent an estimated 85,000 to get the ballot initiative passed (Key 1952) – a sum that translates to 877,000 in 2018 dollars. Democrats and labor unions strenuously opposed the measure (and Taft), citing the number of straight-ticket votes that the party routinely gained in urban areas such as Cleveland.

In the wake of the ballot change, Ohio Democrats found it difficult to find a suitable challenger for Taft. This is not surprising. As we demonstrate below in our empirical analysis, the office bloc ballot enhances the incumbency advantage in part by deterring high-quality challengers. After being turned down by at least two prominent candidates, the Democrats eventually settled on Joseph Ferguson, who was described as "short," and "slight." He also had a "prominent gap in this front teeth." He made such a poor impression on reporters that one remarked, "The smartest thing the Democratic National Committee could do is smuggle their nominee ... out of Ohio and keep him hidden until after the November election" (Patterson 1972, 457).

In the end, Taft easily won reelection in 1950 by more than 400,000 votes. Given the number of moving parts involved and our inability to replay history, it is impossible to produce an exact estimate of the effect of the ballot change on Taft's reelection prospects in 1950, but two things are clear: (1) Taft and his supporters believed that the type of ballot used could alter the outcome. In fact, Taft thought the ballot change was worth up to 200,000 votes in 1950 (Patterson 1972), and (2) they were willing to spend a considerable sum of money to see their proposal enacted.[5]

Election results from 1944 and 1950 lend a great deal of credence to the argument that the office bloc helped separate Taft from the top of the ticket. Figure 4.1 plots the relationship between the Democratic

---

[3] Taft would become Senate Majority Leader in 1953.
[4] If there was any doubt about his ambitions it was resolved when Taft again unsuccessfully sought the Republican nomination in 1952.
[5] The postscript to this story is sad for Taft and his supporters as he died on July 31, 1953, due to pancreatic cancer shortly after becoming Senate Majority Leader.

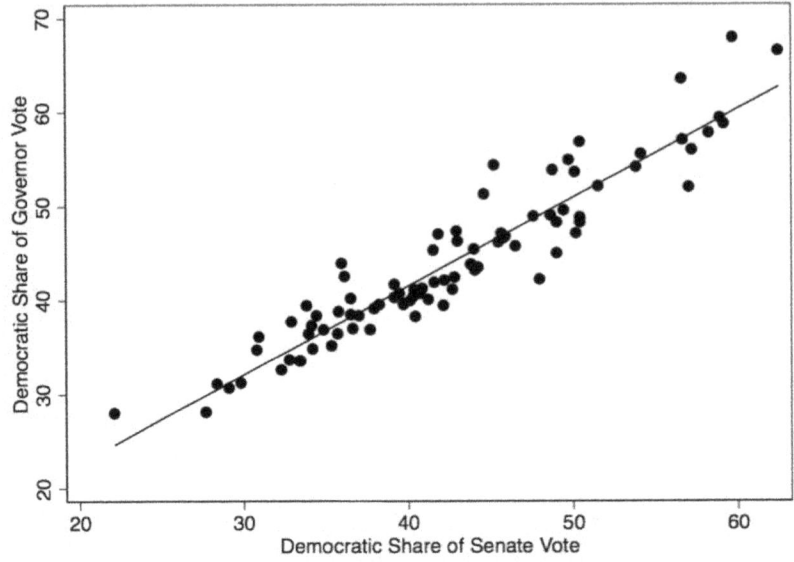

FIGURE 4.1 Relationship between governor and US Senate election, Ohio, 1944

Note: Dots are Ohio counties, line is a bivariate regression line.

share of the vote for Governor and US Senate in 1944 – with the party column – at the county level. The figure shows a tight connection between the two races, the correlation between the vote for Governor and vote for US Senate is 0.94.

In contrast, Figure 4.2 shows a much weaker relationship between the vote for Governor and vote for US Senate in 1950 under the office bloc. The variance within counties is much higher and the vote for Governor is a less predictive of the vote for US Senate. The correlation between the vote percentage in the two races is much weaker than in 1944 at 0.64, which is exactly what we would predict in the wake of the ballot change.[6] As Taft's biographer argues, the change in the ballot benefited Taft in two related ways, (1) by encouraging voters to look at the names on the ballot, Taft gained votes because of his stature, and (2)

---

[6] The reduced correlations between top of the ticket races continued in Ohio post-1950. In 1952, the correlation between the governor's race and the presidential race was 0.83. In 1956, the correlation between the Senate race and the presidential contest was 0.76, it was 0.82 between the governor's race and the Senate race, and was 0.92 for the governor's race and the presidential contest.

4.3 Connecticut: The Power of Defaults

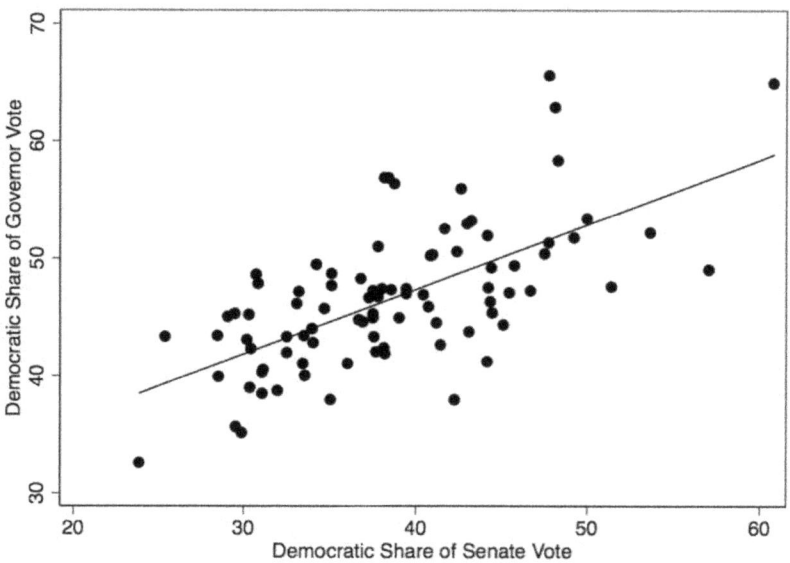

FIGURE 4.2 Relationship between governor and US Senate election, Ohio, 1950

Note: Dots are Ohio counties, line is a bivariate regression line.

the ballot made it more likely that voters would cast a split-ticket ballot. In fact, many speculated that Gov. Lausche himself voted for Taft (Patterson 1972). Taft also managed to win Cuyahoga County, which contains Cleveland, by 23,000 votes in 1950 after losing it by close to 100,000 votes in 1944, which lends some support to Taft's claim that he could break even in the county with the office bloc ballot.

4.3 CONNECTICUT: THE POWER OF DEFAULTS

Connecticut adopted the Australian ballot in 1909, settling on the party column with a straight-ticket option. Voting a straight ticket could be achieved by simply pulling a lever that indicated a straight-ticket ballot. The party lever stayed in place until 1986 when it was removed via a state constitutional amendment. This unusual feature of the Connecticut ballot required voters to first pull a party lever in order to operate a voting machine. After pulling a party lever, the voter could then do nothing else and cast a straight-party vote or they could decide to "cut" individual candidates by moving individual tabs in order to vote a split ticket. One could, in theory, pull the lever for one party, yet vote for all members of the opposing party if they were so inclined.

The lever was not fully removed until 1986, but it had served as a source of conflict at various points throughout the twentieth century. Notably, the "mandatory lever" became highly controversial during the 1960s. A number of lawsuits were filed claiming that the mandatory lever was unconstitutional and spurred many activists to protest the lever policy. One protester, Vivien Kellems, staged a number of protests against the party lever. On Election Day in November 1964, Kellems entered the voting booth at 10:20 a.m. and stayed in the booth for nine hours without casting her ballot. She had told media members that she would not leave the voting booth unless she was "carried out." Unfortunately for Kellems she passed out in the voting booth and had to be revived by onlookers. Her protests continued and ended in arrest after a much shorter time in the voting booth and her lawsuits were unsuccessful, but she did succeed in drawing considerable attention to the party lever issue.[7]

By 1965, there was bipartisan consensus in Connecticut that the party lever should be made optional for voters, but there was considerable disagreement about how to institute the reform. Republicans, who were in the minority party, advocated for a statutory solution, seeking to simply pass a law making the lever optional. Democrats, on the other hand, wanted the change to be more enduring so they sought an amendment to the state constitution. Their reasoning was quite transparent as they argued that the party lever helped support the two-party system and they stated that if the lever was protected only by statute, it could be changed, presumably by Republicans, at any time. Democratic Senator Louis I. Gladstone stated this directly saying that once the lever was optional, "the fear that I have – that the next step will be to eliminate it altogether."[8] Gladstone and the Democrats prevailed in securing a constitutional amendment and for the 1966 election Connecticut had the optional party lever for the first time.

As Figure 4.3 reveals, the results of this change were drastic. Roll-off from the presidential contest to the House contest spiked from 0.68 percent in 1964 with the mandatory lever to 5.22 percent in 1968 as various media accounts reported that some voters found the new voting

---

[7] See "Lever Protesting Vivien Collapses after Sit-in." *Hartford Courant*, November 4, 1964, page 1.
[8] "Battle Seen Building Up On Lever Bill." *The Bridgeport Post*, April 7, 1965, page 73.

FIGURE 4.3 Roll-off by party lever rule, Connecticut

procedure to be confusing.[9] The effects on roll-off were enduring even after Connecticut's voters became acclimated to the new procedure. For the three presidential election years prior to the removal of the mandatory lever, the roll-off rate from the presidential contest to the US House contest averaged a minuscule 0.5 percent. With the switch to the optional party lever the roll-off rate quintupled to an average of 2.82 percent in the three presidential elections after the change.

This result is quite similar to the results that Thaler and Sunstein (2008) report about 401k plan enrollment. When employees are automatically enrolled in employer-sponsored 401k plans but given the option to opt out, most employees remained enrolled; however, when employees have to "opt in" to the plan fewer than half enroll. Note that in both the 401k plan case and the party lever case, the options presented to the individual did not change, only the default choice changed. When the default choice in Connecticut was to vote in the US House election,

---

[9] The sharp spike in roll-off in 1968 followed by a decline in 1972 and subsequent years suggests that there could be diminishing marginal returns to changes in ballot format as voters and politicians adjust to changes in ballot design.

almost all voters chose to do so. However, when the default was not registering a vote for the House contest, fewer voters chose to do so.

This particular example illustrates the power of ballot formats to "nudge" voter behavior. The Connecticut story did not end with the constitutional amendment instituting the optional lever, however. Republicans took control of the Connecticut legislature after the 1984 election and pushed for a constitutional amendment to fully remove the optional lever altogether. Though the effort was led by Connecticut Republicans, the votes to send the amendment to the voters were lopsided – passing the Senate 33–3 and the House 116–28. Connecticut voters narrowly approved the change in 1986, which became effective for the 1988 election (Rose 1992).

Figure 4.3 demonstrates that the effects of removing the lever were stark. The roll-off rate from the presidential contest to the US House election skyrocketed from an average of 2.82 percent in the five elections prior to the change to 8.59 percent in the four elections after the change. Media accounts suggest the change was quite confusing to Connecticut voters with many taking longer to vote, asking where they could find the lever, or voting only the first position on the ballot and thinking that it applied to other contests.[10]

Ironically, the removal of the party lever may have had unintended consequences for some Republicans in Connecticut. As was the case in Ohio with Robert Taft, many Connecticut Republicans thought that straight-ticket voting via the party lever largely benefited Democrats in the state and that Republican incumbents – such as Senator Lowell Weicker – would benefit from voters being forced to make office-by-office choices. Weicker was up for reelection in 1988 – the first federal election in Connecticut without the party lever – and he narrowly lost his reelection bid in 1988 to Democrat Joe Lieberman by a margin of just over 10,000 votes. There was a considerable undervote in the Senate race; 60,000 voters cast a ballot for president, but did not make a choice in the US Senate race, a roll-off rate of more than 4 percent. Given that the Republican presidential candidate, George H. W. Bush won Connecticut, many well-informed political observers in Connecticut argued that most of the undervotes in the Senate race came from Bush voters who likely would have pulled the Republican lever, thus voting for Weicker, if the lever had still been available. As such, some argued that the abolition

---

[10] See "Loss of Party Lever Throws Some for a Loop at Polls." *Hartford Courant*, November 4, 1987, page 42.

of the party lever likely cost Weicker his seat in the US Senate.[11] This episode illustrates that changes in the ballot form often have noteworthy consequences, but these consequences are not always predictable in advance as elections and political circumstances are dynamic.

4.4 NORTH CAROLINA

North Carolina first adopted the Australian ballot in 1909 choosing to go with the party column with a straight-ticket option. As with most of the former Confederate South, North Carolina was a one-party Democratic state for much of the twentieth century. In fact, the Democrats held an uninterrupted majority in the General Assembly from 1898 through 2010. As was true of most southern states, the civil rights reforms of the 1960s were anathema to most North Carolina Democrats. Northern Democrats were ascendant in the national party and had the power to shape the party's national reputation in a more liberal direction. Thus for Democrats in the North Carolina General Assembly, the straight-party option served as a potentially serious electoral liability if the national Democratic Party nominated a northern liberal for president.

Democrats in the North Carolina General Assembly handled this issue in a most unusual manner. Rather than eliminating the party box from the ballot, they chose to formally remove the presidential contest from the slate of races governed by the party box as part of a comprehensive election reform bill in 1967. This meant that a voter could vote a straight ticket for all state, local, and non-presidential federal offices by checking one box, but then had to make a separate choice in order to vote for president. In other words, this clever ballot design helped facilitate dual partisanship in North Carolina. Voters could more easily register their dislike of the national party – by voting for the Republican Richard Nixon – while still voting for Democratic candidates in state and local elections.

This architectural design proved to be fortuitous for North Carolina Democrats. The tumultuous 1968 Democratic National Convention nominated a northern liberal, Vice President Hubert H. Humphrey of Minnesota, while in 1972 the Democratic standard bearer was again a northern liberal, Senator George McGovern of South Dakota. Neither Humphrey nor McGovern fared well in North Carolina with both

---

[11] See "Weicker May Have Second Thoughts about Party-Lever Reform." *Hartford Courant*, November 14, 1988, page 41.

getting less than 30 percent of the vote. Humphrey finished third in the state, behind both Republican Richard M. Nixon and third-party candidate George Wallace in 1968. Nixon's win in North Carolina was the first Republican victory in the state's presidential contest since Herbert Hoover in 1928. In 1972, McGovern was trounced by President Nixon by more than 500,000 votes – the margin between McGovern and Nixon was larger than the total number of votes received by McGovern. Jimmy Carter, of Georgia, narrowly won the state in the 1976, but this would be only Democratic victory in the state between Lyndon Johnson's victory in 1964 and Barack Obama's razor-thin victory in 2008.

Yet, as noted above, the ballot law change helped the Democratic party maintain its General Assembly majority through 2010. Prior to Nixon's landslide victory in 1972, the state's elections director, Alex Brock, pointed out that, "nobody can ride on anybody's coattails because they are disengaged," while Frank Rouse, the state Republican chairman, lamented the change stating, "Sure, it is going to hurt us." The Republican's 1972 gubernatorial candidate considered a lawsuit to challenge the change, but was deterred due to the low probability of success.[12] The law may have helped keep the Democratic majority in the North Carolina General Assembly, but it did have an unusual, likely unintended, consequence – undervote for the office of president. The state's gubernatorial contest drew more votes than did the presidential contest in 1984, 1988, and 1996, but had never done so prior to the separation of the presidential vote from the rest of the ballot.

4.5 PATTERNS OF CHANGE

The three cases discussed earlier clearly demonstrate that the political impact of ballot reforms persisted into the middle part of the twentieth century. Even in an era characterized by higher levels of voter literacy and the decline of urban party machines, we still see considerable evidence that the type of ballot voters encountered in these states had a demonstrable effect on observable political outcomes. We also again see clear examples of strategic actors manipulating the ballot form in order to boost the political careers of ambitious politicians – even if such reforms occasionally backfired on the reformers. In this section, we provide a more comprehensive analysis of state ballot reforms from 1940

---

[12] See "N.C. Ballot Won't Aid Candidate Needing Party Vote for Nixon." *Asheville Citizen-Times*, September 26, 1972, page 2.

TABLE 4.1 *Partisan change in State ballot laws, 1940–2000*

	Non-Congruent	Congruent
Party Limiting	91.18 (31)	85.71 (6)
Party Enhancing	8.82 (3)	14.29 (1)

to 2000 with a focus on ballot roll-off, the incumbency advantage, and representational style in the US Congress.

As in Chapter 3, we begin by considering the political conditions under which states decide to make changes to the form of the ballot. As before, we code each change as either party enhancing – party column, party box; or party limiting – office bloc, party box removal. We again coded each state's political environment as either congruent – same party wins at the presidential and state legislative level – or non-congruent – partisan divide between state and national winners. The results are presented in Table 4.1. One clear finding emerges from these data: most changes in this era were not party enhancing. Fewer than 10 percent of the changes included moving to the party column ballot or adding the party box; this is true for both congruent and non-congruent state governments. These strongly reinforce our argument that most ballot reformers in this era were more concerned with enhancing the fortunes of existing politicians than in securing larger partisan majorities.

In doing so, they adopted ballot forms that helped disconnect the outcome of the top of the ticket races from other partisan races on the ballot. This was done explicitly in Ohio, Connecticut, and North Carolina, but also in the other states. We think this is an under-appreciated force behind the prevalence of divided government in the latter half of the twentieth century. At the congressional level, the turn to incumbent preserving ballot forms clearly benefited the Democratic party. The Democrats held the majority for forty consecutive years in the late twentieth century and maintained majorities in 1972 and 1984, despite landslide presidential elections for the Republican party's candidates. In both 1972 and 1984, Democrats won 189 House seats in districts that the Republican presidential candidate also won.

We explore this more systematically in Table 4.2 below. The dependent variable is the roll-off rate between statewide presidential vote and

TABLE 4.2 *Effect of ballot type on roll-off, 1956–2000*

Variable	Coefficient (Std. Err.)
Office Bloc Box	7.78** (3.06)
Office Bloc No Box	2.17 (3.26)
Party Column No Box	4.31* (2.11)
Year Counter	−0.09*** (0.03)
Presidential Competition	−0.07 (0.08)
Southern State	23.45*** (1.40)
Constant	179.44*** (55.53)
N	598
R^2	0.42

Note: Estimates are from a linear regression model. Standard errors clustered by state in parentheses. State and year fixed effects estimated but not reported. *** = $p \leq 0.01$; ** = $p \leq 0.05$; * = $p \leq 0.10$.

the statewide votes for the US House. The three types of ballots included are: office bloc with a straight-ticket option, party column without a straight-ticket option, and office bloc without a straight-ticket option. The excluded, baseline, format is the party column with a straight-ticket option. The model includes fixed effects for both states and years. The state fixed effects control for time-invariant characteristics of states that may influence ballot roll-off. The year fixed effects control for any election specific variation in ballot roll-off. The model also includes a linear time trend to adjust for the possibility of an independent over time increase in ballot roll-off. The model also controls for statewide competition – measured as the difference in vote share between the Democratic and Republican presidential candidates – and an indicator variable for Southern states given the one-party nature of political competition in that region (Aldrich and Griffin 2017).

The results are presented in Table 4.2. Not surprisingly, Southern states had considerably higher levels of roll-off than did non-Southern states. Beyond that, we do still see a strong effect of ballot type. In keeping with our expectations, roll-off is approximately 4.3 percent higher in states that employed the party column without the party box compared to states with the party column with box ballot format. We also estimate that roll-off is almost 8 percent higher in states using the office bloc with box compared to the party column with box. The only finding in Table 4.2 that is inconsistent with our expectations is that the estimated effect of the office bloc with no box – typically the ballot type most associated with roll-off – is not statistically distinguishable from zero. The estimate is positive, but not as large as we would expect relative to the other ballot types. One possibility for the smaller impact of a pure office bloc ballot is the behavior of politicians under that system. A reasonable conjecture is that incumbent politicians started working harder at reelection activities given the incentives of the office bloc ballot. With incumbents needing to rely less on the parties and more on their own efforts, one might expect them in an office bloc system to redouble their efforts to garner a personal vote. This would also suggest a resulting increase in the incumbency advantage in state using a pure office bloc ballot. The next section examines this possibility.

4.6 THE INCUMBENCY ADVANTAGE

Perhaps no feature of US congressional elections has received more scholarly attention than the electoral advantages accruing to incumbent members of the US Congress. Scholars have developed multiple measures of the incumbency advantage and a litany of potential sources of the advantage, which include, but are not limited to casework, legislative pork, campaign fundraising, the resources of office, and the ability of incumbents to deter high-quality challengers.[13] Though all of the purported sources of the incumbency have some merit, our theory points to ballot type as a potential source of variation in the magnitude of the incumbency advantage.

As we discussed in Chapter 2, voters are apt to look for the "right" answer when making choices on the ballot. Incumbents benefit from this in at least two potential ways. First, one of the most important

---

[13] See Roberts and Carson (2011) for a partial review of the voluminous literature.

advantages that an incumbent possesses over his or her challenger is name recognition. Incumbents receive more news coverage than do challengers, can typically outspend their challengers on yard signs and advertisements, and can send franked mail to their constituents highlighting their congressional achievements at no cost to themselves. As such, voters are much more likely to recognize an incumbent's name on the ballot as compared to most challengers. We know that voters often choose a name that is most recognizable even if they have little or no personal experience with that person, which works to the benefit of incumbent candidates. Second, serving as the incumbent allows members of Congress to develop a reputation or "name brand" with their constituents. Incumbents who successfully complete case work, take positions that please voters, and claim credit for their accomplishments can and do build up goodwill with voters (Mayhew 1974).

These benefits of incumbency should be amplified by ballot nudges that encourage voters to make office-by-office choices and depressed by ballot forms that encourage straight-ticket voting. This is exactly why Senator Taft's supporters pursued ballot reform in Ohio. Taft enjoyed high name recognition and had developed a sterling reputation in the state, which would work to his advantage if voters were nudged to make office-by-office choices on the ballot. The mechanism at work with Taft in Ohio likely existed throughout the country, thus we expect the incumbency advantage to be larger in states that employ the office bloc ballot and/or in states that do not have a straight-ticket provision on the ballot.[14]

We assess the effects of ballot type on the incumbency advantage in the US House in two ways. First, we estimated models of the incumbency advantage using the two equation approach employed by Cox and Katz (1996). The first equation generates an estimate for the "direct" effect of incumbency, which refers to the effects of elements such as resources and the personal vote and the "quality effect" of incumbency, which refers to the advantage that an incumbent receives by simply being an experienced candidate. This equation is estimated via ordinary least squares (OLS),

$$DTP_{it} = \alpha + \beta_1 DQA_{it} + \beta_2 DTP_{it-1} + \beta_3 DQA_{it-1} + \beta_4 I_{it} + \beta_5 I_{it-1} + \beta_6 P_{it} + \beta_7 P_{it-1} + \sum_t \beta_{8t} Year_t + \epsilon_{it} \quad (4.1)$$

where DTP refers to the Democratic percentage of the two-party vote in the current election, DQA refers to the Democratic Quality Advantage,

---

[14] This is consistent with what Carson and Roberts (2013) found for the pre-1944 era.

4.6 The Incumbency Advantage

coded 1 if a Democratic incumbent or quality candidate ran against an amateur Republican, 0 if a Democratic quality candidate ran against a quality Republican or if two amateurs faced off, and −1 if a Republican incumbent or quality candidate ran against an amateur Democrat. I refers to the presence of an incumbent, coded 1 for a Democratic incumbent, 0 for an open seat, and −1 for a Republican incumbent. P refers to the party defending the seat, coded 1 for Democrat and −1 for Republican. I is the estimated direct effect of incumbency and DQA is the estimated quality effect. This equation was estimated separately for all four ballot types: office bloc without box, office bloc with box, party column without box, and party column with box.

The results are presented in Table 4.3 and they are in keeping with our expectations. The estimates for the direct effect of incumbency are consistently larger in the absence of the party box on the ballot, in party column states the direct effect is more than 2.5 percent larger when there is no party box, and the effect is 1.2 percent larger in office bloc states that do not have a party box. The estimates for the quality effect of incumbency also meet our expectations, with effect being the largest for the office bloc with no box ballot and the smallest for party column with box ballot type.

The second equation measures the "scareoff" effect of incumbency, which refers to the extent to which an incumbent being in the race deters the entry of an outparty quality candidate to challenge the incumbent. This equation is estimated via OLS.

$$DQA_{it} = \alpha + \beta_1 DTP_{it-1} + \beta_2 DQA_{it-1} + \beta_3 IR_{it} + \beta_4 IR_{it-1} \\ + \beta_5 P_{it} + \beta_6 P_{it-1} + \sum_t \beta_{7t} Year_t + \epsilon_{it} \quad (4.2)$$

The estimated scareoff effect IR is then used to calculate the total incumbency advantage (IA) according to following formula: $IA = I + (DQA * IR)$. The scareoff equation was estimated separately for all four ballot types. The results, which are presented in Table 4.4, reveal that the scareoff effect is significantly larger in office bloc states than in party column states. Office bloc ballots by design focus voters more on the individual candidates and less on their party affiliations, thus making it easier for incumbent candidates to develop a "personal vote" (Cain et al. 1987) and insulate themselves from national party tides. These results suggest that strategic politicians may well understand that the office bloc ballot enhances the incumbency advantage and respond by having a higher threshold for emergence in elections decided with this ballot method.

TABLE 4.3 *Estimating the direct and quality effect of incumbency*

Variable	OB-No Box	OB-Box	PC-No Box	PC-Box
Lagged Democratic Vote	0.62***	0.66***	0.70***	0.70***
	(0.01)	(0.03)	(0.02)	(0.01)
Incumbent Running	6.41***	5.23***	7.34***	4.75***
	(0.41)	(0.88)	(0.72)	(0.42)
Lagged Incumbent Running	−1.05**	−0.80	−2.69**	−1.41**
	(0.34)	(0.75)	(0.59)	(0.37)
Party Defending Seat	−2.72**	−3.45**	−3.23**	−1.88**
	(0.43)	(0.91)	(0.76)	(0.44)
Lagged Party Defending Seat	0.49	0.24	0.92	0.73**
	(0.28)	(0.66)	(0.50)	(0.33)
Democratic Quality Advantage	3.81***	3.68***	3.19***	2.45***
	(0.25)	(0.55)	(0.47)	(0.25)
Lagged Democratic Quality Advantage	−0.10	0.53	0.40	−0.06
	(0.25)	(0.55)	(0.47)	(0.25)
Constant	23.82***	17.94***	21.17***	26.25***
	(2.07)	(4.65)	(2.45)	(1.41)
N	3456	698	1097	3112
R^2	0.85	0.86	0.87	0.83

Note: Coefficients are from a linear regression model with standard errors in parentheses.
*** = $p \leq 0.01$; ** = $p \leq 0.05$; * = $p \leq 0.10$.

Taken together the results in Tables 4.3 and 4.4 clearly suggest that the magnitude of incumbency advantages varies by ballot type. The two ballot types that boost incumbents the most are the office bloc with no box (8.04 percent) and the party column with no box (8.46 percent), this is consistent with our expectations regarding the party box. When the box or lever is not present, voters are more apt to cast a split ticket as they decide who to vote for in a contest-by-contest manner. As was the case with Senator Taft of Ohio, incumbents can leverage their name recognition advantage to gain votes when voters are not using the party box or lever. In contrast, the incumbency advantage is not as strong in the office bloc with box (7.03 percent) and particularly the party column with box (5.63 percent) ballot types. Split-ticket voting is reduced under these ballot types and incumbents are less able to benefit from voters making office-by-office choices.

4.6 The Incumbency Advantage

TABLE 4.4 *Estimating the "Scareoff" effect of incumbency*

Variable	OB-No Box	OB-Box	PC-No Box	PC-Box
Lagged Democratic Two Party Vote	0.01*** (0.001)	0.01*** (0.002)	0.01*** (0.001)	0.009*** (0.001)
Lagged Democratic Quality Advantage	0.08*** (0.02)	0.10*** (0.04)	0.14*** (0.03)	0.13*** (0.02)
Incumbent Running	0.43*** (0.03)	0.49*** (0.06)	0.35*** (0.05)	0.36*** (0.03)
Lagged Incumbent Running	−0.02 (0.02)	−0.05 (0.05)	−0.02 (0.04)	−0.001 (0.03)
Party Defending Seat	0.12*** (0.03)	0.14** (0.06)	0.16*** (0.05)	0.15*** (0.03)
Lagged Party Defending Seat	0.03* (0.02)	0.06 (0.05)	−0.001 (0.03)	0.05** (0.02)
Constant	−0.27* (0.14)	0.16 (0.33)	−0.59*** (0.16)	−0.07 (0.10)
N	3456	698	1097	3112
R^2	0.73	0.80	0.76	0.73

Note: Coefficients are from a linear regression model with standard errors in parentheses.
*** = $p \leq 0.01$; ** = $p \leq 0.05$; * = $p \leq 0.10$.

Our second method of assessing the effect of ballot type on the incumbency advantage involves individual-level survey data drawn from responses to the American National Election Studies (ANES). At its core, the incumbency advantage occurs because voters choose to vote for their incumbent member instead of a candidate for the other party, which they would presumably do if the seat were open. If enough voters make this choice in a given district, then that incumbent will see his or her vote share boosted over what a non-incumbent member of the same party would expect to gain in an open seat race.[15]

We assess this by coding whether or not an ANES respondent reported casting a split ticket in presidential election years by voting for the respondent's incumbent House member and the presidential candidate of the opposite party. This variable, coded 1 if the respondent reported voting this way, is the dependent variable for the logistic regression model

---

[15] This is somewhat similar to the logic of the sophomore surge and retirement slump measures of the incumbency advantage.

TABLE 4.5 *Ballot type and split-ticket voting*

Variable	Coefficient (Std. Err.)
Moderate	0.05 (0.06)
Strong Party ID	−0.37*** (0.09)
Weak Party ID	0.14* (0.08)
Leaner Party ID	0.11 (0.09)
Office Bloc Box	0.05 (0.11)
Office Bloc No Box	0.12** (0.06)
Party Column No Box	0.18* (0.08)
Constant	−2.20*** (0.11)
N	16935
Log-likelihood	−6423.57
$\chi^2_{(18)}$	252.34

Note: Estimates are from a logit model. Split ticket between president and US House is the dependent variable. Year fixed effects estimated but not reported. *** = $p \leq 0.01$; ** = $p \leq 0.05$; * = $p \leq 0.10$.

presented in Table 4.5. Independent variables in this model include a measure of whether or not the respondent reports being a ideological moderate,[16] three indicator variables that correspond to the strength of the respondent's reported party identification, and indicator variables for ballot type.[17]

---

[16] We code someone as a moderate if they place themselves at 4 on the liberal/conservative 7-point scale.
[17] The party identification variables are coded such that respondents who report being "Strong Democrats" are coded identically to those who report being "Strong Republicans;" the same is true for weak identifiers and leaners. Pure independents are the excluded category.

The results presented in Table 4.5 further confirm our expectations. As we would expect, respondents who report having a strong party identification are less likely to cast a split-ticket ballot than are respondents who report a weaker affiliation with a political party. Substantively, the probability of a respondent who reports having a strong party identification voting a split ticket is 0.05 less than someone reporting any other strength of party identification. We also find strong evidence to suggest that ballot type can in fact "nudge" voters to behave differently. We do not find any consistent differences between the office bloc and party column forms of the ballot, but we do find that the presence or absence of the party box is a strong predictor of split-ticket voting. For voters who experience a ballot without the party box, we see that the probability of reporting a split-ticket vote increase by 0.02. In terms of substance, these results suggest that the impact of ballot type on split-ticket voting is approximately 40 percent of the magnitude of the strength of party identification. This is in keeping with our expectations and further confirms the Campbell and Miller (1957, 299) argument that you cannot understand how a voter votes without understanding the type of ballot being employed.

Taken together these results shed light on one of the most discussed changes in American legislative elections in the latter part of the twentieth century – the growth of the incumbency advantage. Ballots with a straight-ticket option suppress the incumbency advantage compared to ballots that nudge voters to make office-by-office choices. The average incumbency advantage is approximately 30 percent larger in districts without the straight-party option (8.25 percent) than it is in districts with it (6.33 percent). These results are quite consistent across our entire data series, but the distribution of ballot type is not. In the 1940s, more than half (56.4 percent) of the US House was elected on a ballot that contained the party box. This percentage hovered around 50 percent through the 1970s, before falling to 41.8 percent in the 1980s, and 34.4 percent in the 1990s. By the year 2000, fewer than one-third of House members were elected on ballots with the party box and only 16.6 percent were elected on the party column with box ballot, which is the ballot type that is least helpful in boosting incumbent vote shares. Ballot type was certainly not the sole cause of the rise in the incumbency advantage. Declining partisanship in the electorate contributed, as did the fact that the major parties did not always draw major distinctions between themselves on policy issues. We think it is likely that the political environment of this era both facilitated the growth of the incumbency advantaged and facilitated the adoption of ballot laws that protected incumbents. Yet, we think our results clearly demonstrate that ballot type itself was an independent contributor to the increase in the incumbency advantage.

4.7 REPRESENTATIONAL STYLE

Our focus to this point has been on why politicians choose certain ballot forms and how those choices can influence election outcomes, but we also have reason to expect ballot form and legislative strategy to be related. That is, given that incumbent politicians typically seek to remain in office, we would expect them to pursue strategies inside the legislature that help them pursue that goal. For example, one can think of democratic representatives as choosing between two broad legislative strategies (Cain et al. 1987; Carey and Shugart 1995; Cox 1987). One strategy is to rely on the visibility of the national party label and mobilization efforts of co-partisans for reelection. As in strong party systems, what an individual legislator does in office has less impact relative to what the national party label does for him or her. Voters cast ballots based principally on their judgments about which party would govern best, not on the individual policy promises of individual legislators. As a result, legislators have less reason to pursue independent policy initiatives and tailor a distinct position-taking record for local consumption. A second strategy involves trafficking in the politics of local opinion. Here the independent initiative of legislators becomes critical. What individual legislators say and do matters more for voters as voters depend less on party labels and more on the "name brand" of the incumbent politician. In this type of system we contend that members will work to sponsor legislation, make speeches, and craft a roll-call record that appeals to the median voter in their district (Bernhard and Sulkin 2018; Sulkin 2005, 2011; Wawro 2010).

Legislators, however, face a trade-off over how much effort they can devote to these position-taking activities relative to other activities. Finite resources prevent them from devoting all of their scarce time to position-taking. We know that institutional rules, such as a district magnitude, affect how members choose to allocate their time (Taylor et al. 2018). Likewise, we expect ballot formats to influence the relative effectiveness of these differing legislative strategies (Carson and Sievert 2015; Wittrock et al. 2008).

As we have noted throughout the book, ballots without a party box diminish the influence of the overall party label and this is particularly true when the ballot form is office bloc. The office bloc no box format requires voters to work through the ballot, making individual choices office-by-office. As a result, what legislators do in office should carry more weight. Moreover, relying on the popularity of candidates at the top of the ticket becomes a much riskier strategy. This suggests that the office bloc should place a premium on independent initiative relative to the party column. As such, we expect members to rely to a greater extent on their personal and position-taking characteristics in office bloc systems (minus a straight-ticket option).

By contrast, in states with a party column with box format, the pressures to take public positions and to pursue independent legislative initiatives should be reduced. In party column states, the fates of candidates are more closely tied to the success of presidential and gubernatorial candidates at the top of the ticket. An unpopular presidential administration or a lackluster presidential nominee can hurt the electoral chances for down ballot candidates, irrespective of their individual effort. Similarly, a popular presidential or gubernatorial candidate can aid candidates of the same party through coattail effects. Because their electoral fates are subject to public views of the national party label, one would expect less pressure for party column legislators to craft a distinct personal reputation, and therefore less pressure to spend time on position-taking activities.

In short, there is good reason to suspect an influence of ballot formats on the legislative strategies of representatives. In office bloc with no box states, where the influence of the party label is diminished, members need to rely to a greater extent on their personal and position-taking characteristics. In states with a party column ballot with box, the pressures to take individualized public positions and to pursue independent legislative initiatives should be lessened.

If we are correct, then we should find legislators from office bloc states pursuing legislative strategies that are more focused on improving their individual reputation in the district.[18] There are many aspects

---

[18] While we cannot confirm that members are fully aware of the ballot format in each state, we do know that members reside in and vote in the districts they represent, thus they have the opportunity to be exposed to information on ballot type on a biennial basis.

to democratic representation, but we focus on three pivotal, and measurable, features here: sponsoring legislation, effectiveness at lawmaking, and roll-call voting.

4.7.1 Sponsoring Legislation

Bill sponsorship is one of the quintessential tools by which members can take positions on issues. By writing and introducing a bill, members can take public stands on the direction they think existing policy should move and bring new issues to light. Bill sponsorship provides members with abundant opportunities to stake out positions. Moreover, members have direct control over sponsorship.

To examine the connection between ballot laws and bill sponsorship, we estimated a count model predicting the number of bills sponsored by House members from 1946 through 2000. The data on individual bill sponsorship comes from the Congressional Bills Project (Adler and Wilkerson 2013). The dependent variable is the number of bills sponsored by a representative during a Congress.[19]

The key independent variables are a series of indicator variables capturing ballot format. For the analysis, we divided ballot formats into the same four ballot types we have analyzed throughout – office bloc with box, office bloc no box, party column no box, and party column with box. The model also includes controls for the number of years the member served in the House, whether the member was in the majority party, and their margin of victory in the preceding election. In estimating a model over this time period, one also needs to account for changes in the rules regarding co-sponsorship of legislation. Prior to the 91st Congress, House members were prevented from signing on as co-sponsors of a bill. The ban on cosponsorship resulted in numerous duplicate bills as legislators sought to claim credit for similar ideas (Thomas and Grofman 1993). Beginning in the 91st Congress (1969–1971), representatives were allowed to cosponsor bills. The new rule initially limited the number of cosponsors to twenty-five. The House removed this cap starting in the 96th Congress (1979–1981). To account for the impact of these rule changes on sponsorship proclivity, we included a dummy variable for the 91st through 95th Congress (1969 to 1978), and then another dummy variable for the 96th Congress and after (1979 to 2000). The years before

---

[19] The model includes both public and private bills. We have also run the analysis with just public bills. The ballot variable remains positive and significant.

1969 serve as the omitted category. Because the dependent variable is a count, we estimated the model using a negative binomial regression. This modeling strategy accounts for the likely possibility of overdispersion in the dependent variable.[20]

The results presented in Table 4.6 strongly support the hypothesis that representatives respond to the incentives emanating from their electoral structure. Our expectation was that members elected from an office bloc ballot would sponsor more legislation. In Table 4.6 this is what we see. The coefficient on both office bloc variable is positive and the office bloc without party box is statistically significant. Substantively, being elected under the office bloc with no box ballot form is associated with a 5.2 increase in the number of bills sponsored as compared to a member elected under the party column with box ballot type. To put this in context, for the 96th–107th Congresses, the average number of bills sponsored by a member of the House was 13.7, so the office bloc without box is associated with a 38 percent increase in bill sponsorship, which is of comparable magnitude to the difference in majority versus minority status in the chamber, which is quite substantial.[21]

In the next section, we study the effect of ballot format on the extent to which US House members are able to shepherd the legislation they sponsor through the legislative process.

4.7.2 Legislative Effectiveness

Whereas simple bill introductions require minimal effort from members and no collective action, to actually move legislation through the process takes some combination of skill, institutional position, and effort (Volden and Wiseman 2014). Volden and Wiseman (2014) find that a number of factors help explain why some members are more successful or effective than others in shepherding the bills they sponsor through a legislative process that is biased toward inaction on the overwhelming majority of measures. Factors leading to increased effectiveness include components

---

[20] The model also includes state and Congress fixed effects and the standard errors were clustered by member.

[21] One concern with these findings might be that legislators from office bloc states differ from party column states for some un-modeled reason that happens to correlate with ballot type. To address this we also ran our model including individual legislator fixed effects. This adjusts for any time-invariant characteristics of legislators that may influence their propensity to sponsor legislation. In this estimation the office bloc coefficient was again positive and significant, and the magnitude virtually unchanged.

TABLE 4.6 *Ballot type and bill sponsorship*

Variable	Coefficient (Std. Err.)
Office Bloc No Box	0.22*** (0.07)
Office Bloc With Box	0.02 (0.08)
Party Column No Box	−0.10 (0.07)
Majority Party Member	0.21*** (0.03)
Seniority	0.04*** (0.004)
Margin of Victory	0.0005 (0.0004)
91st–95th Congresses	1.82*** (0.33)
96th–106th Congresses	1.25** (0.58)
Intercept	1.02** (0.51)
N	12121
Log-likelihood	−43880.95
χ^2	8647.29

Note: Cell entries are negative binomial maximum likelihood coefficients. State and Congress fixed effects estimated by not reported, standard errors clustered by member in parentheses. *** = $p \leq 0.01$; ** = $p \leq 0.05$; * = $p \leq 0.10$.

of institutional position such as being in the majority party, serving in the party leadership, or serving in a committee leadership post. Additionally, members who have previous experience working in a professionalized state legislature have more success moving their proposals through the legislative process. This suggests that legislative effectiveness is a product both of legislative skill or experience and the ability to leverage one's institutional position to gain positive outcomes on legislative proposals.

In this section, we analyze the relationship between ballot type and legislative effectiveness. As we noted earlier, ballot types that focus the attention of the voter more on candidate attributes and less on the party

4.7 Representational Style

label typically induce members to engage in behavior that promotes their own name brand to their constituents. Thus we have little doubt that members running on these type of ballots would prefer to be more effective legislators, all else equal. If more of a member's proposals successfully move through the legislative process, the member will have more items to claim credit for when attempting to build goodwill with the electorate (Mayhew 1974). However, unlike a position as a committee chair, the type of ballot that a member runs for Congress on provides, in and of itself, no institutional advantage for a member to use to gain positive action on a legislative proposal. We certainly think that the type of ballot would affect a member's incentives, but that may or may not be associated with success or failure.[22] An association between ballot type and legislative effectiveness then would likely be capturing the effects of member effort on legislative effectiveness rather than inherent skill or institutional position.[23]

We explore the connection between ballot type and legislative effectiveness in Table 4.7. To do so we simply add our measures of ballot type to the legislative effectiveness model presented in Volden and Wiseman (2014).[24]

The results in Table 4.7 largely mirror those found in Volden and Wiseman (2014). However, we do find a strong, positive association between ballot types that incentivize members to develop a personal reputation and that member's legislative effectiveness score. As compared to the party column ballot with a party box, both the office bloc no box, and the party column no box ballots are positively associated with increased legislative effectiveness scores. This suggests that ballot type does perhaps induce members to spend more time and resources on legislating if they are forced to run for reelection under a ballot type that does not include a party box. The substantive effect is not as large as being a committee chair, but it is larger than those associated with demographic characteristics of the members. These results confirm our expectations about the relationship between ballot type and legislative effectiveness

---

[22] The labor market incentivizes the authors to be able to throw a baseball at a high rate of speed and accuracy with our left hands, but neither of us has succeeded in doing so.
[23] Of course, it is also possible that ballot type induces certain types of individuals to run or not run for Congress.
[24] Volden and Wiseman (2014) track member bill proposals and score them based on how far they progress through the legislative process. These scores are then combined into a measure of legislative effectiveness for each member. This score has a mean of 1 for each Congress. For the congresses we analyze the minimum value is 0.01, the median is 0.42, and the maximum is 18.68.

TABLE 4.7 *Ballot type and legislative effectiveness*

Variable	Coefficient	(Std. Err.)
Lagged Effectiveness Score	0.47***	(0.03)
Seniority	0.03*	(0.007)
State Legislative Experience	−0.10*	(0.06)
State Legislative Experience x Legislative Prof.	0.41**	(0.19)
Majority Party	0.31***	(0.05)
Majority-Party Leadership	0.31**	(0.14)
Minority-Party Leadership	−0.03	(0.06)
Speaker	−0.31	(0.24)
Committee Chair	2.12***	(0.20)
Subcommittee Chair	0.54***	(0.06)
Power Committee	−0.13***	(0.04)
Distance from Median	−0.15	(0.09)
Female	0.07*	(0.04)
African American	−0.19**	(0.09)
Latino	0.04	(0.08)
Vote Share	0.03***	(0.01)
Vote Share^2	−0.0002**	(0.0001)
Size of Congressional Delegation	−0.002	(0.002)
Office Bloc No Box	0.18***	(0.05)
Office Bloc with Box	0.04	(0.05)
Party Column No Box	0.11**	(0.05)
Constant	−0.99**	(0.40)
N	6098	
R^2	0.56	
$F_{(21,1293)}$	89.95	

Note: Cell entries are linear regression coefficients. Standard errors clustered by member in parentheses. *** = $p \leq 0.01$; ** = $p \leq 0.05$; * = $p \leq 0.10$.

and help us tell a more complete story about how ballot type affects voters, election outcomes, and the type of representation the citizens receive.

In the next section, we turn our attention to the effect of ballot format on the positions adopted by representatives. In particular, we examine how ballot formats influence the incentives of legislators to support the president on roll-call votes.

4.7.3 Roll-Call Voting

One of the more difficult strategic problems that members of Congress face is how to craft a roll-call voting record. Members must balance myriad competing influences including key constituencies, party leaders, interest groups, the president, and their own personal preferences. Making the task more difficult is that political challengers and single-interest groups rarely consider a member's record in totality; instead members live in constant fear that taking the "wrong" position on an issue could lead to electoral defeat (Mayhew 1974).

There is considerable evidence that members' fears are well-founded. One of the more noteworthy instances of this occurred in 1993, when Marjorie Margolies-Mezvinsky, a freshman member from Pennsylvania, was pressured by then President Bill Clinton to support his position on the 1993 budget reconciliation bill. Margolies-Mezvinsky, who was elected on an office-bloc ballot, had voted against Clinton's position on the budget on two previous occasions, but on the conference report her vote turned out to be pivotal. As Smith et al. (2013, 399) detail, the vote closed with the Democrats down two votes. First one member who had yet to vote cast a no vote, then Pat Williams (D–MT) changed his vote to yes. At that point,

[A]ll eyes fell on Margolies-Mezvinksy, who was being ushered to the front desk by a group of her colleagues. The Republicans chanted, "Goodbye, Marjorie," referring to her reelection prospects if she voted against them. She signed the green card to [change her vote] vote to yes, and the Speaker gaveled the vote closed.

The Republican chants proved to be prophetic as Margolies-Mezvinsky subsequently lost her reelection bid in 1994.[25]

A number of studies have demonstrated that Margolies-Mezvinksy's story is not uncommon. Voting with one's party or president *too much* can cause a member electoral harm (Canes-Wrone et al. 2002; Carson et al. 2010; Nyhan et al. 2012). On the other hand, supporting a popular president's legislative agenda can be electorally advantageous for members. Caro (1982) recounts in exquisite detail how pledging support to President Franklin D. Roosevelt's New Deal agenda was instrumental in Lyndon Johnson's first election to the US House of Representatives in 1937. Similarly, Kernell (1997) details how President Ronald Reagan's

---

[25] This story continued to take interesting twists. First, Margolies-Mezvinsky's son, Marc, married Clinton's daughter, Chelsea, in 2010. Second, she sought to return to the House to represent the 13th district of Pennsylvania in 2014, with the help and support of former President Clinton, but lost in the primary.

popularity and his affinity for "going public" was key in winning budget battles with a Congress controlled by members of the opposite party. On a more systematic level, scholars such as Bond and Fleisher (1990) and Edwards (1990) have identified factors such as party, ideology, and region as key to understanding why members of Congress support the president's agenda.

In this section, we consider the relationship between the type of ballot a member is elected on and the member's roll-call voting record. To do so we analyze the percentage of Congressional Quarterly's "Key Votes" in which a House member votes for the president's announced position.[26]

As we noted earlier, we expect members to pursue more self-interested representational strategies when they are elected under an office bloc ballot and more party-oriented strategies when elected under a party column ballot. With respect to support for the president's position on roll-call votes, we expect members to be more cognizant and hence responsive to the popularity of a president when considering whether or not to align themselves with him on roll-call votes under the office bloc ballot. For members elected under the party column ballot, we expect their support of the president's agenda to be less responsive to the president's popularity within their district. Ideally, we would test our hypotheses by measuring a president's popularity in each district at the time of each vote, but such granular data do not exist. Instead, we rely on aggregate measures of support and presidential popularity in each district. Our independent variables are the member's margin of victory in the previous election, the president's margin of victory in the member's district for the previous election, and an indicator variable for whether the member and the president are of the same party. We fit this model for each of our four ballot types. The results of our analysis are presented in Table 4.8.[27]

Not surprisingly, one of the most important predictors of a member's presidential support score – across all ballot types – is his or her party affiliation. Members who are of the same party as the president have a support score that is more than 10–12 percent higher than members of the opposing party. We also find that members who won their seats with

---

[26] Data taken from the Presidential Data Archive and can be accessed at http://presdata.tamu.edu. We converted the annual data to run for the length of an entire Congress.
[27] We employed the same robustness checks for these models as we employed for the sponsorship analysis. The relationship between exposure to the office bloc ballot and roll-call voting remained the same, even after adjusting for any mean group differences between office bloc and party column legislators.

4.7 Representational Style

TABLE 4.8 *Ballot type and presidential support*

Variable	OB-No Box	OB-Box	PC-No Box	PC-Box
Member's Margin of Victory	0.14***	0.11	0.06	0.13**
	(0.05)	(0.11)	(0.07)	(0.06)
Presidential Margin of Victory	1.10***	1.06***	1.00***	0.92***
	(0.05)	(0.04)	(0.07)	(0.02)
Same Party as President	12.62***	10.12***	13.74***	12.42***
	(0.80)	(1.79)	(1.46)	(0.89)
Constant	31.64***	51.05***	51.54***	62.08***
	(10.85)	(5.07)	(7.21)	(3.51)
N	3491	664	1019	2919
R^2	0.37	0.49	0.47	0.31

Note: Cell entries are linear regression coefficients. Standard errors clustered by member in parentheses. *** = $p \leq 0.01$; ** = $p \leq 0.05$; * = $p \leq 0.10$.

a larger margin, who may consider themselves more electorally secure, are more likely to support the president's position on roll-calls and this relationship is statistically significant for the office bloc no box format and the party column with box format.

To us, the most interesting variable in these analyses is the president's margin of victory in a member's district. We would expect members to be most attuned to this variable under the office bloc with no box ballot format. Members and the president are not as linked electorally under this format so members should be less likely to vote with an unpopular president. Members will unlikely be harmed for voting with a popular president, but we would expect them to be more responsive to the president's political standing in their district when deciding whether or not to support the president's position. In contrast, members elected under the party column with box format are much more electorally linked to the president. It would not be surprising to see members elected under this ballot to support presidents of their party, regardless of the president's political standing in the district. If the president succeeds then the member can expect positive electoral effects, whereas a failed presidency can drag now even a popular House member. The results in Table 4.8 confirm our expectations. The president's margin of victory is positive and significant across all ballot types, but the coefficients are the largest for the office bloc no box format and smallest for the party column with box format, which suggests that members are more responsive to the president's political standing in the office bloc with no box format.[28] Ballot type is certainly not as strong a predictor as the member's party affiliation or the underlying partisan composition of the district – it ranges from negligible in close districts to 2–3 percent in districts with a 10–15 point presidential margin of victory – but our results consistently show that members elected under an office bloc ballot have roll-call records that are more finely tuned to the underlying political atmosphere in the district than are members elected on a party column ballot.

4.8 CONCLUSION

The strategic problem facing politicians of the mid-twentieth century differed dramatically from that facing politicians today. With a less partisan electorate and weakened party organizations, ambitious politicians had to find ways to secure election without relying solely on the campaign activities and mobilization efforts of local party organizations. One institutional solution to this problem was to redesign ballot architecture to elevate individual politicians above party labels in the minds of voters. In places like Ohio and Connecticut, strategic politicians refashioned the ballot to nudge voters away from simply voting a straight ticket by default. In North Carolina, local Democrats reworked ballot architecture to electorally insulate themselves from a national Democratic Party that had become firmly pro-civil rights.

The result not only changed the nudges that voters received, but also altered the downstream incentives of candidates and incumbent officeholders. Ballot designs that deemphasized party labels led to increases in the incumbency advantage. Politicians in states with a pure office bloc ballot chose electoral strategies that emphasized their personal accomplishments and downplayed their national party label. Representatives elected in states with an office bloc ballot, without a straight-ticket option, sponsored substantially more legislation than those elected in states with a party column or a straight-ticket option. They were also more effective at turning these proposals into laws. Similarly, representatives in office bloc states, minus a straight-ticket option, were more sensitive to local district opinion when casting roll-call votes. In short, office bloc legislators trafficked more in the politics of opinion than did their counterparts from party column and/or straight-ticket states.

[28] The coefficient differences are statistically significant according to a Chow test.

4.8 Conclusion

By the beginning of the twenty-first century, the strategic problem of politicians had once again shifted. Today each party has a reasonable shot at gaining control of national political institutions; something that was rarely true for congressional elections between 1956 and 1994 (Lee 2016). At the same time, elections have become nationalized and congressional parties have also sharply polarized ideologically. Within Congress, each party contigent has become much more ideologically homogenous internally and distinct from the other party. The result of these many related changes for voter behavior has been a deemphasis away from the personal characteristics of candidates and a reemphasis on parties as semi-unified teams of politicians (Jacobson 2015).

Against this backdrop, party politicians have once again turned to ballot architecture in the bid for political power. These large scale changes in the national electoral environment have redirected the attention of politicians toward using ballot architecture for strictly partisan gain. Chapter 5 turns to an examination of the battles over ballot architecture that are roiling statehouses and influencing elections throughout the country.

5

Ballot Architecture in the Contemporary Partisan Era

The 2000 presidential election between Democrat Al Gore – the incumbent Vice President – and Texas Governor Republican George W. Bush had one of the most dramatic endings of any election in American history. Polling in the final weeks of the race was tight and most observers considered the election "too close to call" heading into election day. However, as the early returns were reported, it was looking like a good night for Vice President Gore. Major media outlets "called" the critical state of Florida for Gore early in the evening based on exit poll data and early election returns. With Florida in Gore's column, it was difficult to construct a winning electoral map for Governor Bush. Bush and his brother Jeb, the Florida Governor, protested that the network call of the state was premature, if not incorrect. A few hours later the major networks agreed and "un-called" the state. Much later in the dizzying evening, Florida was again called – this time for Bush – only to be un-called yet again in the wee hours of the following morning. Adding to the confusion, Gore called Bush to concede the election at one point in the evening only to call back later and revoke his concession.

For the first time in decades, Americans awoke on the morning after the election not knowing who would be their next president. However, two things were clear: (1) the outcome in Florida would decide the presidency, and (2) the margin of victory in Florida would be razor-thin. Florida election law called for an automatic recount in the case of an election decided by less than 1 percent of the vote and this contest easily met that threshold. The final election night count had Bush up by less than 1,800 votes out of more than 5.9 million votes cast.

As the recount commenced, attention focused on two things that few Americans had thought much about prior to the election. The first

FIGURE 5.1 "Hanging" chad

Note: Figure provided by Douglas W. Jones, Department of Computer Science, University of Iowa.

was "chads." Many Florida counties used punchcard-style ballots that required a voter to use a stylus to punch out a perforated piece of cardboard or "chad" in a machine-readable card to register their vote. Votes were tabulated by machines reading missing chads in ballots as votes for the candidate in that ballot position. Many of the machines (and voters!) were old and not all chads were completely dislodged from the ballot.

The terminology used to describe these chads would have been humorous had the stakes not been so high. There were "hanging" chads that were dislodged on two of the four corners of the ballot (see Figure 5.1), "dangling" chads that were attached on only one corner, "punctured" chads that had a hole in the center of them but were otherwise attached, and the "pregnant" chads that bulged out the backside of the ballot but that had no holes or separation from the ballot (see Figure 5.2). Much of the legal and political controversy that emanated from the recount was over the issue of chads, but all centered on the question of how to determine the intent of the voter and what standards to use in determining intent. For example, is a pregnant chad indicative of a voter who wished to cast a ballot but failed to do so due to physical weakness and/or equipment failure, or is it indicative of a voter who considered voting for a candidate but changed his/her mind before displacing the chad?

The second was the innocuous-sounding "butterfly" ballot. As we noted in Chapter 2, some ballots in Palm Beach County were designed with candidate names in two columns, one on the left of the center line and one on the right. The vote selection holes ran down the middle of these two columns (see Figure 2.1). The most important feature was that the ballot position alternated columns, so the first name in the left column (George W. Bush) corresponded to the first ballot hole, the first name in

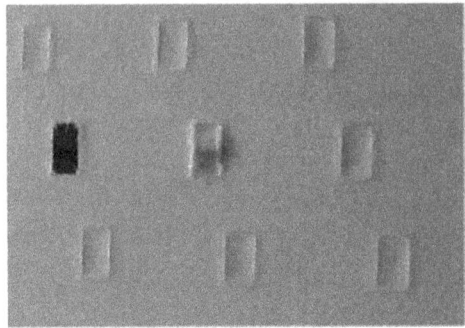

FIGURE 5.2 "Pregnant" chad

Note: Figure provided by Douglas W. Jones, Department of Computer Science, University of Iowa.

the right column (Pat Buchanan) corresponded to the second ballot hole, and the second name in the left column (Al Gore) corresponded to the third ballot hole. Unfortunately for Vice President Gore, approximately 2,000 voters in Palm Beach County mistakenly punched out the second ballot hole (vote for Buchanan) instead of the third ballot hole (vote for Gore).

After an extended legal battle that culminated with the US Supreme Court decision in *Bush* v. *Gore*, Bush was declared to be the victor in Florida by a mere 537 vote margin, which secured the presidency for him. With an election decided by such a slim margin, myriad things could have affected the final outcome. However, the evidence analyzed by political scientists is clear in stating that Vice President Gore would have won the presidency if the butterfly ballot had not been used in Palm Beach County, FL(Wand et al. 2001).

Our focus here is not on the outcome of presidential elections, but we contend that the 2000 election controversy helped change the dynamics of ballot reform in multiple related ways. First, it highlighted the importance of seemingly mundane election administration issues such as ballot design, voting equipment, and standards for counting ballots. This issue went from something few had ever considered to something that literally decided the outcome of a presidential election. Second, it prompted Congress to get involved in election administration in hopes of preventing another Florida fiasco. In 2002, Congress passed the Help America Vote Act (HAVA), which authorized spending up to $650 million to improve poll access for voters with disabilities and upgrade obsolete voting technology in states and localities – including punch card machines.

The passage of HAVA resulted in many states making changes to voting equipment and ballot type that were not directly related to partisan political goals or incumbency protection. Finally, the razor-thin margin of the 2000 election signaled an escalation of an era of heightened partisan competition for Congress, the presidency, and many state legislatures.

In many ways, the post-2000 era mirrors the Progressive Era we discussed in Chapter 3. The strategic problem politicians confront is once again how to win partisan majorities at the state and national level in a polarized and electorally competitive environment. The sweeping Republican victory in the 1994 congressional elections ended a four-decade period in which the partisan control of the US House was rarely, if ever, in doubt heading into an election year. Majority party margins in both chambers have been razor-thin since 1995 and both parties have gone into almost all election cycles with a realistic chance of winning or losing majority control. At the same time, the two major parties have never produced more polarized voting records, which has made the opportunity costs of winning and losing congressional majorities incredibly high (Lee 2016).

Moreover, voters have also altered their behavior in this era of renewed partisan conflict (Hetherington 2001). As voters have sorted themselves into parties that match their ideologies, fewer voters than ever are casting split-ticket ballots across all strengths of party identification and all ballot forms (Levendusky 2009; Jacobson 2015). As such, elections are increasingly "nationalized" with outcomes highly correlated across offices and the personal vote component of the incumbency advantage has declined sharply (Jacobson 2015). As Figure 5.3 demonstrates, the correlation between the House vote and the presidential vote in a district has increased drastically since 2000, reaching an all-time high in 2012.

The combination of narrow margins and increasingly predictable voting behavior has once again highlighted the importance of voter mobilization and turnout to election victories. Much like in the late nineteenth century, parties and candidates now invest as much, if not more, on turnout and mobilization as they do on persuasion. These efforts can and do focus on traditional and newly discovered methods such as canvassing, phone calls, and psychological shaming in order to encourage or discourage certain individuals and groups from voting. However, as we demonstrate in this chapter, it can be much more efficient for a dominant state legislative party to enact changes to election laws in order to encourage or discourage certain groups from voting. States have pursued

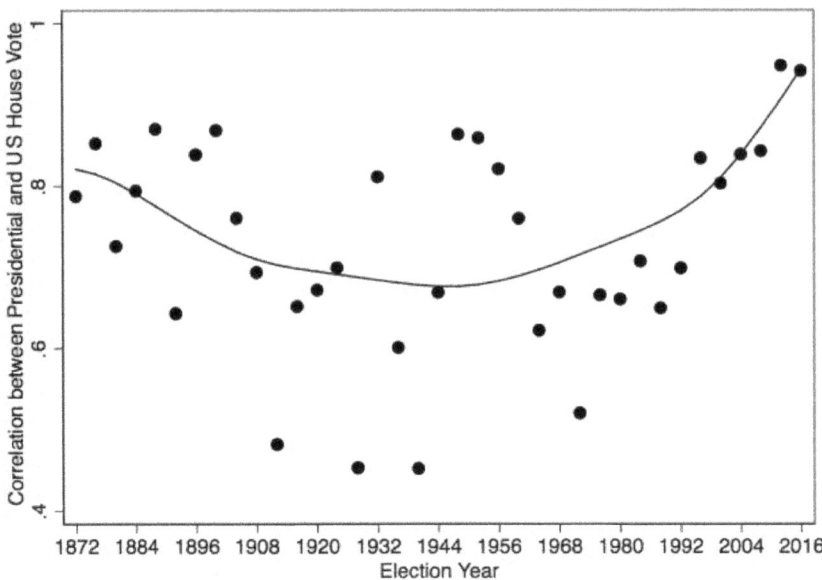

FIGURE 5.3 Correlation between presidential and US House vote, 1872–2016

Note: Points are individual election year correlations. Line is a lowess smoother.

a wide range of reforms including strict voter identification requirements, automatic voter registration, and, of course, the format of the ballot. Since 2000, ten states have passed legislation that removed or would remove the straight-ticket option from the ballot in their state.[1] Most of these changes have been highly contested, partisan enactments with Republican-controlled legislatures voting to remove the straight-ticket option from the ballot. As we demonstrate later, in many of these states straight-ticket voting was heavily concentrated in areas with large minority populations – areas that vote predominately for the Democratic party in most elections.

Our approach in this chapter is quite different than we have taken in the previous two chapters. We have a shorter time period and thus fewer changes in ballot type to analyze, so we forego broad analyses of patterns across all states. We do, however, have very detailed data on straight-ticket voting patterns in a few states for a limited time period. These

---

[1] The ban in Texas goes into effect in 2020. Michigan's was enjoined by a court ruling in 2016, was allowed by a court ruling for 2018, and was overturned by voters during the 2018 election.

data allow us to provide a more fine-grained analysis of the effect of ballot design changes in these states. In the next two sections, we analyze changes in Michigan and North Carolina in great detail. In both cases, we have detailed data on usage of the straight-ticket option before the law was changed, as well as data on ballot roll-off and turnout after the laws were changed. We also provide analysis of ballot design changes in Iowa and West Virginia. We have less data on these two states, but we think they provide insight into the limits of ballot design changes on elections and election outcomes.

5.1 MICHIGAN

Michigan first adopted the Australian ballot in 1891 by instituting a party column with party box ballot style. Since that time, there have been three formal attempts to remove the party box from the Michigan ballot. All three were originated by the Michigan legislature and all three were ultimately thwarted by the Michigan electorate.

In 1964, a Republican-controlled Michigan legislature passed a bill to replace the party column with box ballot style with the office bloc with no box style. The votes in the Michigan legislature were heavily partisan and the arguments were quite familiar to readers of our case studies from Chapter 3. Republicans did not enjoy being weighted down by popular Democratic presidential candidates – Lyndon Johnson would secure more than 61 percent of the vote in Michigan in 1964. Democrats and labor leaders led the fight against the new ballot, arguing that it would lead to longer lines and increased voter confusion.[2] This effort was overturned, however, by a referendum vote in the state. Proponents of keeping the party box were able to put the removal question on the ballot by collecting more than 100,000 signatures. In November 1964, the state's voters decided emphatically to keep the existing ballot style, party column with party box, by a 66 percent to 34 percent margin.[3]

Similarly, in 2001, a Republican-controlled Michigan legislature again passed a bill to remove the party box from the ballot, but it was met by the same fate as the 1964 bill. Democrats, noting that Michigan has one of the longest ballots in the country, again argued that it would cause long lines in polling places and discourage some voters from participating.

---

[2] See "Ballot Change Brews Fight," *The Detroit Daily Press*, August 16, 1964.
[3] The Michigan Constitution provides a referendum option for voters to overturn acts of the legislature.

Republicans countered that the elimination of the party box would encourage more people to vote in non-partisan races.[4] Once again, proponents of the party box were able to put the removal on the ballot and Michigan's voters again chose to keep the party box in November 2002, this time by a 60 percent to 40 percent margin.

As the vote totals on two referenda suggest, the party box is quite popular in Michigan and has been for several decades. In the 2016 elections, 51.6 percent of Michigan's voters chose to use the party box for voting, which is in line with rates from other recent election years.

Despite the popularity of the straight-ticket provision, the Republican-led legislature again sought to remove it in 2015. The partisan intent seemed clear, as not only was the party box popular with Michigan's voters, there was also no clear administrative reason to remove it. In fact, the clerks who testified in front of legislative committees considering party box removal argued just the opposite. According to the House Legislative Analysis, "City and county clerks testified that the average wait time to vote in Michigan was already 22 minutes, and that this measure could double that wait." Clerks also testified that the number of spoiled ballots would increase, causing still longer lines and more frustration. If the doubling of the average Michigan wait time to 44 minutes had occurred, it would have pushed average Michigan wait time to almost 50 percent over the recommendation of the EAC that wait times be less than 30 minutes (Ansolabehere and Stewart, III 2015).

Despite opposition from majorities of Michigan voters and the unanimous opposition of city and county clerks, the Michigan legislature successfully passed a bill removing the party box in December of 2015. They also attempted to make the bill referendum proof by attaching a $5 million appropriation to the bill.[5] The politics of this bill were quite compelling but the final outcome was not surprising. At the time the bill passed, Republicans had unified control of state government in a state that regularly voted for Democratic presidential candidates. In fact, no Michigan Democratic legislator supported the removal of the party box.

---

[4] See "Plan to Halt Straight-Ticket Voting Raises Concerns," *Lansing State Journal*, November 27, 2001.

[5] The referendum policy in Michigan has never applied to appropriations bills. This was expanded considerably by a state Supreme Court decision in 2001, *Michigan United Conservation Clubs* v. *Secretary of State* that held that any bill with an appropriation was immune from referendum. Thus the legislature can make any policy referendum proof by attaching any appropriation to the bill, whether the monies are ever spent or not.

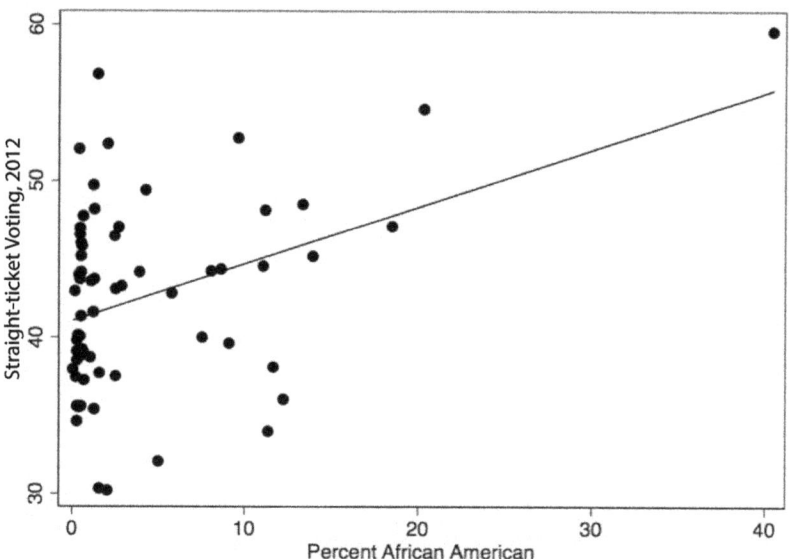

FIGURE 5.4 Straight-ticket voting and African-American population, Michigan, 2012

Note: Dots represent Michigan counties; line is a bivariate regression line.

Overall, the Republican party had secured more votes from the party box than had the Democrats for the three years in which data are available (2012, 2014, and 2016). However, as Figures 5.4, 5.5, and 5.6 demonstrate, the counties in Michigan with the highest proportion of voters choosing to use the party box were urban areas with a large proportion of African-American voters. Not coincidentally, these counties also were some of the strongest performing Democratic counties in the state.[6]

During the floor debate on this bill, its supporters claimed that they wished to adopt a policy that would encourage more "deliberative voting," and increase participation in non-partisan races. Neither of these arguments hold up under careful scrutiny, however. First, the correlation between straight-ticket voting and roll-off on statewide non-partisan Supreme Court races was negative in 2012, 2014, and 2016. That is,

---

[6] Wayne County is both the largest county in Michigan and the one with the largest proportion of African-American residents. In some senses, it is an outlier in the analyses that follow. Omitting it from our analyses dampens some of the effects reported subsequently, but does not change the substantive conclusions of our analyses.

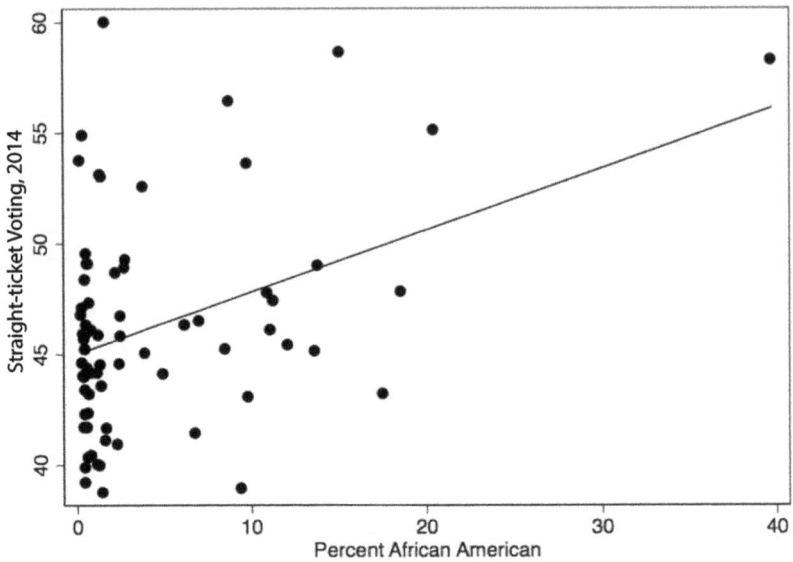

FIGURE 5.5 Straight-ticket voting and African-American population, Michigan, 2014

Note: Dots represent Michigan counties; line is a bivariate regression line.

counties with higher levels of straight-ticket voting had higher levels of ballot completion in non-partisan races. Second, documents produced during the legal battle against the bill provide a rare insight into what members of the legislature were trying to accomplish in eliminating the party box and how they attempted to navigate the politics of the bill's passage.[7] These documents uniformly and repeatedly reveal partisan motivations for the elimination of the party box and provide no mention of increasing "deliberative voting." For example, former Michigan Republican Party Chairperson and current US Secretary of Education, Betsy DeVos, sent the following email to Michigan Senate Majority Leader Arlan Meekof on the passage of Senate Bill 13 that called for the elimination of straight-ticket voting in Michigan.

---

[7] Michigan's ban on the straight-ticket voting was contested in the federal court case *Michigan State A. Philip Randolph Institute, Common Cause, Mary Lansdown, Erin Comartin, and Dion Williams vs. Ruth Johnson*. One of the authors, Roberts, served as an expert witness in this case on the side of the plaintiffs.

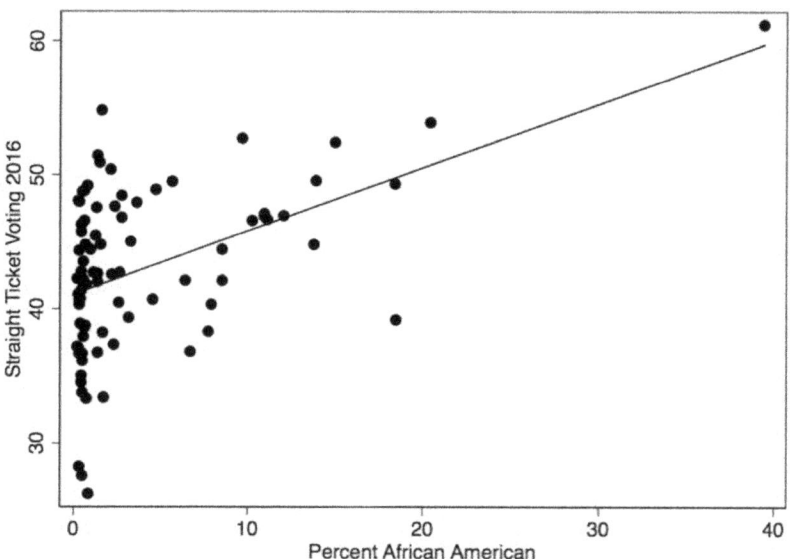

FIGURE 5.6 Straight-ticket voting and African-American population, Michigan, 2016

Note: Dots represent Michigan counties; line is a bivariate regression line.

Hi *Arlan,*

Just want to congratulate you and thank you for your leadership and perseverance on the elimination of straight-ticket voting! While only time will bear out the importance of this for those running "down ticket," the implications are significant!

Gratefully,

To which Meekof responded, "Thank you Betsy! I am proud of our accomplishments."

Meekof had much to be proud of, as he had successfully thwarted an effort by the Chair of the Michigan House Elections Committee, Lisa Posthumous Lyons, to "tie-bar" or append her bill that would have provided for "secure no-excuse absentee voting" (SNRAV) to the bill eliminating the party box (STE). Representative Lyons was leaving the Michigan House and was running to be the Kent County Clerk and Register of Deeds. During the debate on party box removal in the House, she was able to append the SNRAV bill to the bill banning the party box. She indicated in emails to other clerks throughout the state that she expected to see longer lines at polling places if the party box was removed and she hoped that SNRAV would help mitigate these lines. However, Republicans were bitterly divided on the question of whether to connect the two bills.

Representative Lyons and many on the House elections committee favored appending the SNRAV bill to the straight-ticket elimination bill, while many in the Senate and the State Republican Party Chair, Ronna Romney McDaniel, opposed it. Lyons testified that she thought removing the party box was good policy, but it was also clear she thought it was tricky political terrain, emailing an associate: "I don't need to be sold on elimination [of] straight ticket, but we have a real PR problem on our hands right now, so we need do it while providing ways to negate the 'long line' arguments." She later texted Bill Zaagman, chief lobbyist for Michigan Association of County Clerks and Michigan Association of Municipal Clerks, "So ... are you making sure all your clerks are telling house members that straight ticket elimination is a nightmare without no-reason absentee voting?" She later argues to Zaagman that, "... besides being good policy together, SNRAV gives the GOP members good "cover" on the PR/politics hits of STE."

Representative Lyons appears to have been quite frustrated by the intra-party battle over her SNRAV bill. At one point during the debate she sent a text message to her father, who happened to be an aide to Michigan Governor Rick Synder, "I finally had to have Kevin [Speaker of the Michigan House] call Ronna [GOP Chair] and tell her all her calls to members trashing no-reason was killing straight ticket elimination." She also forwarded a news article that suggested that the Michigan Senate would break the two bills apart to her sisters with the message, "Here's a sneak peek of the planned screwing I am supposed to receive." She did keep up her efforts though and in doing so highlighted some of the partisan motivations behind eliminating the party box. During the debate she encouraged the Ottawa County Clerk, Justin Roebuck, to try to persuade Senate Majority Leader Arlan Meekof to keep the two bills together, writing,

> I'd reach out to Arlan and encourage him to let the tie-bar on straight ticket elimination to secure no reason stand. Tell him from your perspective as a former party operative, you understand STE [elimination], but you also know that SNRAV will not hurt republicans or help democrats. Tell him that together you think these bills are good policy, and both very important.

It seems that Lyons was working to convince her Republican colleagues that adding SNRAV would not boost the fortunes of the Democratic party and thus undermine the Republican gains they hoped to secure through the removal of the party box. It is not clear why Lyons's colleagues in the Senate were so fervently opposed to her SNRAV bill.

In her deposition, former State Republican Party chair, Ronna Romney McDaniel made it clear that she thought removal of the party box would enhance the fortunes of the Republican party. She repeatedly pointed out that, as party chair, she found it difficult to recruit high-quality Republican candidates for down-ballot races in many areas due to potential candidates being concerned that the "top of the ticket" would dominate and make it difficult to win a race. Similarly, she noted that she struggled to get down-ballot candidates to raise money and mount a vigorous campaign again due to candidates thinking their efforts would be subsumed by the top of the ticket. She noted that this issue had been particularly difficult in recent presidential election years due to the "Obama juggernaut," by which she seemed to be referring to the efforts made by the two Obama campaigns to mobilize Democratic voters.

While we are not in a position to evaluate Romney McDaniel's claims with regard to candidate recruitment and candidate effort, the data we have do illustrate the down-ballot effects of party box usage in Michigan. There is a strong, negative correlation between levels of straight-ticket voting in a county and the roll-off rate for statewide, partisan contests in Michigan. Figures 5.7, 5.8, and 5.9 demonstrate this relationship for the 2012, 2014, and 2016 elections. Across all three elections we have analyzed, ballot completion rates are much higher in counties that have higher utilization of straight-ticket voting. Further, the counties with the highest levels of party box usage are heavily Democratic. In 2012, Barack Obama won Wayne County, the largest county in Michigan and the one with the highest proportion of party box usage, with 73 percent of the vote. Given these data, it seems clear that Betsy DeVos's prediction likely had merit. Removal of the party box in Michigan would likely benefit Republicans running down ballot as we would expect to see fewer Democratic voters completing their ballot in down-ballot races.

In fact, in some circles the bill to eliminate the party box in Michigan was known as the "Weiser Bill" as it was backed by current Michigan Republican Party chair Ron Weiser. Weiser had unsuccessfully sought a seat on the University of Michigan Board of Regents previously and purportedly thought that removing the straight-ticket option from the ballot

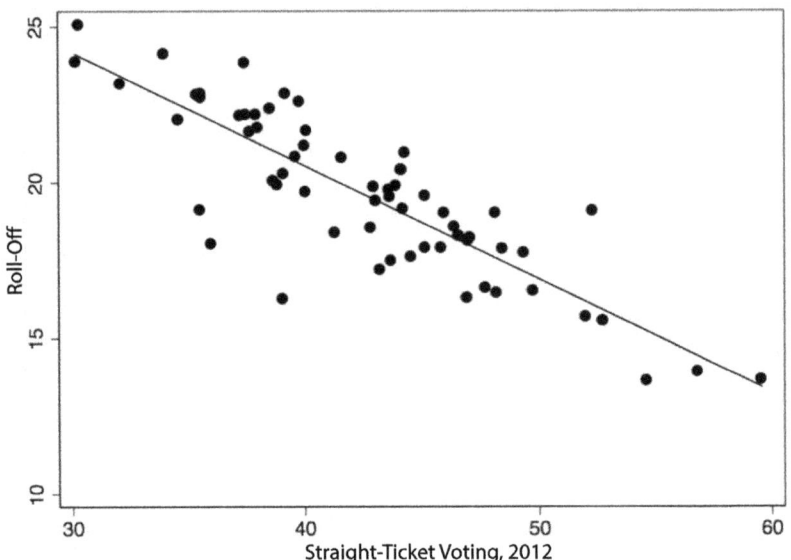

FIGURE 5.7 Straight-ticket voting and ballot roll-off, Michigan, 2012

Note: Dots represent Michigan counties; line is a bivariate regression line.

would enhance his chances of securing a seat on the Board of Regents in 2016. Weiser was successful in his 2016 bid even with the party box still in place.

5.1.1 Michigan Postscript

The legal battle against the bill played out over a more than two-year period. The Michigan legislature intended for the straight-ticket removal to be in effect for the 2016 general election, but a federal judge enjoined its application in July 2016 pending the outcome of the trial in the case. Case proceedings concluded in early 2018 and in August 2018 the judge in the case overturned the law on the grounds that it violated the equal protection clause of the 14th Amendment and Section 2 of the Voting Rights Act. The judge agreed with the plaintiffs that eliminating straight-ticket voting in Michigan would produce longer lines, lower levels of ballot completion, and reduced turnout, and that these effects would disproportionately affect African-American voters in Michigan.[8] However,

---

[8] The case title was *Michigan State A. Philip Randolph Institute, Common Cause, Mary Lansdown, Erin Comartin, and Dion Williams v. Ruth Johnson*

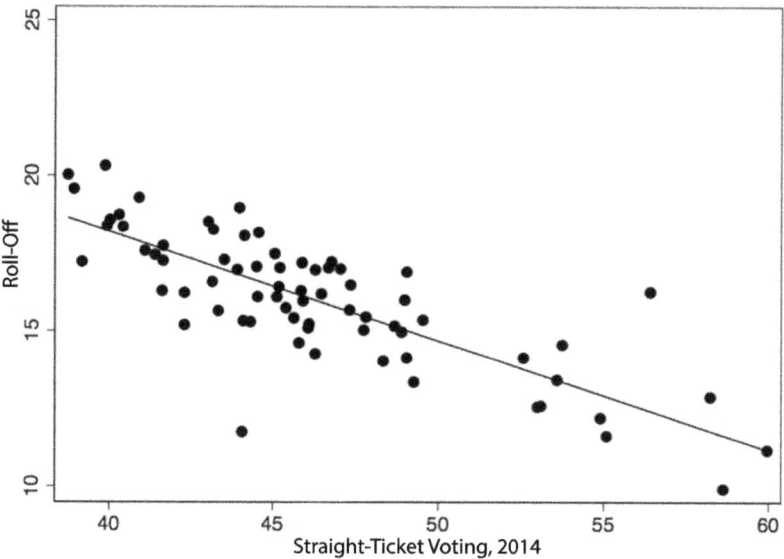

FIGURE 5.8 Straight-ticket voting and ballot roll-off, Michigan, 2014

Note: Dots represent Michigan counties; line is a bivariate regression line.

this ruling was stayed by the 6th Circuit Court of Appeals pending appellate review, which had the effect of allowing the straight-ticket ban to go forward for the 2018 general election in Michigan.

Thus for the 2018 election, there was no straight-ticket option on the Michigan ballot. There were, however, three ballot proposals on the ballot, one of which dealt directly with the straight-ticket voting issue. Michigan Proposal 3 sought to amend the Michigan constitution to authorize no-reason absentee voting, to require a straight-ticket voting option on the ballot, provide for automatic voter registration, and allow same-day voter registration. This proposal passed overwhelmingly, garnering the support of 66.9 percent of Michigan voters. Thus, for the third and likely the final time, Michigan's voters overturned their legislature to reinstate the straight-ticket option on the general election ballot.[9]

The 2018 election in Michigan presents an intriguing angle on the effects of ballot reform as it was conducted without the straight-ticket

---

[9] The initiative called for the straight-ticket provision to be added to the state constitution, so it cannot be removed by statute. Adoption of the proposal effectively mooted the federal court case against the straight-ticket ban.

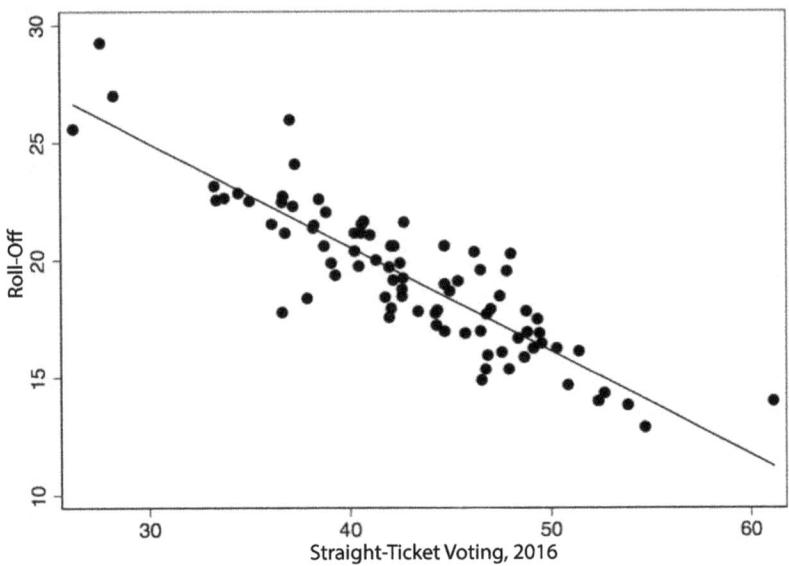

FIGURE 5.9 Straight-ticket voting and ballot roll-off, Michigan, 2016

Note: Dots represent Michigan counties; line is a bivariate regression line.

option. However, in addition to the typical mix of offices on the Michigan ballot, there were three ballot initiatives at the end of the ballot. One dealt with marijuana, one dealt with redistricting, and one was the aforementioned item that explicitly dealt with the straight-ticket voting ban. In general, we would expect the removal of the straight-ticket option to produce an increase in ballot roll-off, which, as Table 5.1 reveals, we do see for lower-level statewide offices. In 2014, for example, the roll-off rate for the State Board of Elections race was 12.11 percent compared to 15.98 percent in 2018. Similarly, the University of Michigan Board of Regents contest had a 14.04 percent roll-off rate in 2014 and increased to 19.09 percent in 2018.

The largest changes in roll-off from 2014 to 2018 occurred in counties that previously had higher levels of straight-ticket voting, as we would expect. It stands to reason that the change in ballot format would have the largest effect in counties that previously employed the straight-ticket option. Without the straight-ticket option in 2018, the data suggest that many voters who had previously voted a straight ticket may have cast an incomplete ballot in 2018. However, in terms of absolute roll-off

5.1 Michigan

TABLE 5.1 *Ballot roll-off in Michigan, 2014, 2016, and 2018*

	2014 Election	2016 Election	2018 Election
Attorney General	2.07	–	4.46
Secretary of State	2.51	–	1.78
State Board of Education	12.11	14.37	15.98
University of Michigan Regents	14.04	17.53	19.09
Michigan State University Trustees	14.11	17.42	19.29
Wayne State University Governors	16.19	19.23	21.44

level in 2018, it was *lower* in counties that previously had higher levels of straight-ticket voting. We think this is directly related to the ballot proposals that voters were asked to consider.

The ballot proposals were placed at the end of the ballot and had very low levels of abstention or roll-off.[10] Support for Proposal 3, which dealt directly with straight-ticket voting, was strong throughout the state, but it was positively correlated with previous levels of straight-ticket voting, which indicates users of the straight-ticket option were likely strong supporters of Proposal 3. Though we lack direct evidence on this point, we think it is likely that the presence of Proposal 3 at end of the ballot induced many previous users of the straight-ticket option to cast complete ballots even in the absence of straight-ticket voting. As Figure 5.10 demonstrates, there is a very strong negative relationship between support for Proposal 3 in a county and roll-off in the State Board of Election Race.[11]

The Michigan example illustrates both the potential and the limits of using ballot laws to pursue political gain. Michigan Republicans entered 2019 with six-seat margins in both state legislative chambers despite being outvoted by Democratic party by more than 300,000 votes in 2018 elections and losing all statewide offices on the ballot. Gerrymandered districts no doubt helped Michigan Republicans and it is clear that the straight-ticket voting ban was designed to help them. However, they ran into two barriers that politicians in the Progressive Era did not have to confront. The Voting Rights Act of 1965 delayed implementation of the straight-ticket ban. Furthermore, modern campaign and communication

---

[10] The roll-off rates were 0.35 percent for Proposal 1, 2.91 percent for Proposal 2, and 2.1 percent for Proposal 3.
[11] State Board of Election is used as an illustrative example; similar relationships hold throughout the 2018 Michigan ballot.

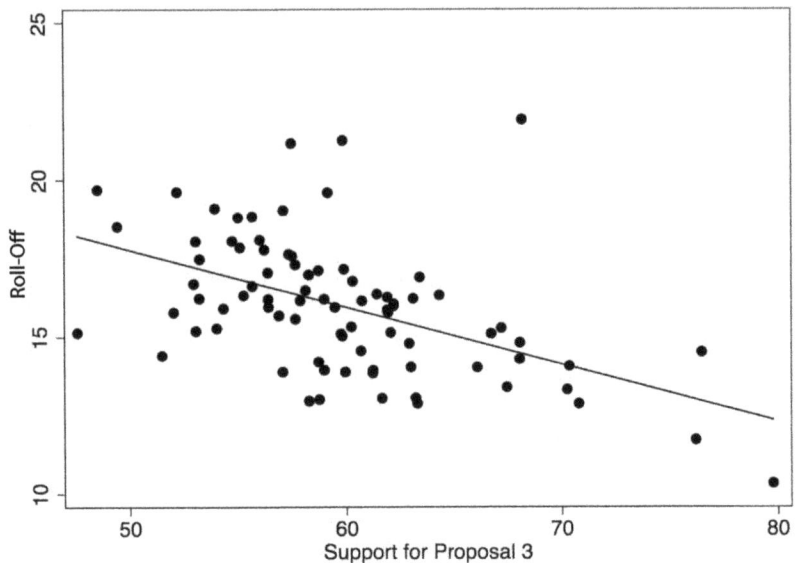

FIGURE 5.10 Proposal 3 and roll-off in Michigan, 2018

Note: Dots represent Michigan counties; line is a bivariate regression line.

tactics combined with Michigan's direct democracy features to give angry voters an outlet to counteract the legislature. Proposal 2 outlawed the kind of partisan gerrymandering that allowed the Republicans to hold the majority post-2018, while Proposal 3 liberalized voter registration laws, provided for easier absentee voting, and restored straight-ticket voting. Despite their best efforts to the contrary, Michigan Republicans will now be forced to run under a ballot format and election law regime that will be less than advantageous to them moving forward.

5.2 NORTH CAROLINA

As noted in Chapter 1, North Carolina enacted a comprehensive voter reform bill in 2013 that was largely invalidated by federal courts. However, one of the most significant changes to North Carolina election practice that was not part of the federal case against the law was the elimination of the straight-ticket voting option. The 2014 election was the first one held in North Carolina without a straight-ticket voting option since North Carolina adopted the Australian or secret ballot in 1909.

Since 2014, voters have been required to mark the ballot for each race individually even if they wish to vote for all of one party's candidates.

As is the case in Michigan, the straight-ticket option was quite popular with North Carolina voters. In the 2010 midterm election, 1.1 million or 43.6 percent of North Carolina voters chose the straight-ticket option. In the 2012 election, the numbers were even higher, with 2.55 million out of 4.47 million voters (57.2 percent) casting a ballot by choosing the straight-ticket option.

As was also true in Michigan, straight-ticket voting was not uniformly popular across the state's hundred counties. In some counties, as few as 33 percent of voters chose to vote a straight ticket in 2012, but in others more than 75 percent of voters chose the straight-ticket option. There was a strong, positive correlation (0.66) between the racial composition of counties in North Carolina and the degree of straight-ticket voting. As illustrated in Figure 1.1, counties with larger African-American populations had much higher levels of straight-ticket voting in 2012. It was also true that counties with higher levels of straight-ticket voting had higher levels of Democratic voting. As Figure 5.11 demonstrates, there was a

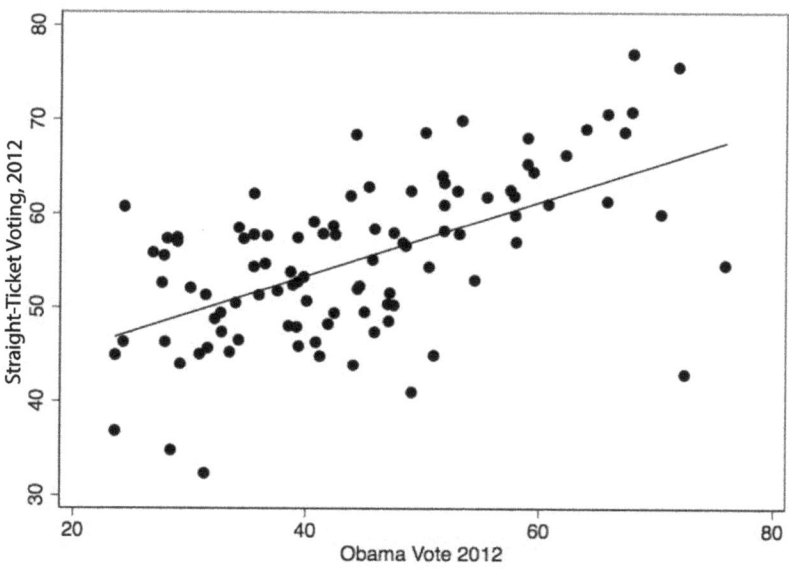

FIGURE 5.11 Obama vote and straight-ticket voting, North Carolina, 2012

Note: Dots represent North Carolina counties; line is a bivariate regression line.

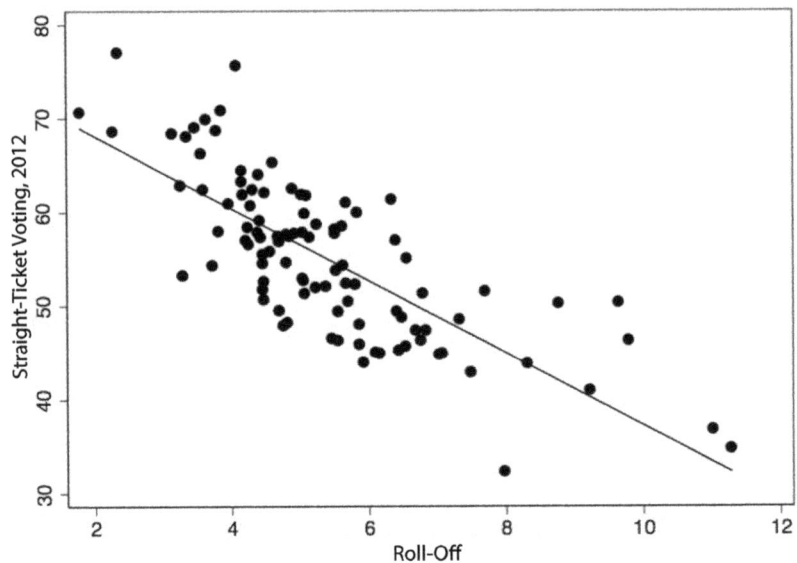

FIGURE 5.12 Roll-off and straight-ticket voting, North Carolina 2012

Note: Dots represent North Carolina counties; line is a bivariate regression line.

strong, positive correlation (0.58) between Obama's 2012 vote percentage and the proportion of North Carolina voters choosing to use the straight-ticket option.

There was also a strong, negative correlation (−0.77) between the rate of straight-ticket voting in a county and ballot roll-off in statewide, partisan races. As Figure 5.12 later demonstrates, counties with higher levels of straight-ticket voting had much lower levels of ballot roll-off than did counties with lower levels of straight-ticket voting.

Taken together, these results demonstrate a clear relationship between the racial and political composition of North Carolina counties, straight-ticket voting, and the level of ballot roll-off in statewide partisan races. Counties with large African-American populations had higher utilization of the straight-ticket voting option in 2012. Counties with high levels of straight-ticket voting utilization had significantly lower levels of ballot roll-off in statewide partisan races. Not coincidentally, these counties also had higher than average levels of support for Barack Obama in 2012. Thus the political motives for North Carolina Republicans were clear: removing the party box from the North Carolina ballot was likely to lead to longer lines, increased roll-off, and decreased voter turnout – all concentrated in areas that were more likely to vote Democratic.

5.2.1 Effects of Eliminating Straight-Ticket Voting in North Carolina

The first two elections conducted in North Carolina without the straight-ticket option for voters were the 2014 and 2016 elections. The following analysis assesses the effects of the elimination of the straight-ticket voting option on ballot roll-off and voter turnout for these two election years.

5.2.2 North Carolina 2014

The 2014 North Carolina election was conducted in a midterm election year, so none of the council of state offices were on the ballot. The only statewide partisan race on the North Carolina ballot in 2014 was the US Senate contest between Republican Thom Tillis and Democrat Kay Hagan. All ballots in the state also included partisan races for the US House, North Carolina Senate, and North Carolina House, but the ballot length is considerably shorter in midterm years than presidential years in North Carolina.

Ballot roll-off tends to increase as ballot length increases, yet the available data indicate a strong association between the removal of the straight-ticket voting option and ballot roll-off in 2014 – despite the short ballot. In 2010, the average level of roll-off from the US Senate contest to the North Carolina House contest in North Carolina counties was 8.3 percent, while in 2014 it was 17.79 percent. Contests for the North Carolina House vary from district to district in terms of candidate quality, candidate funding, and other factors, but these data suggest that the elimination of straight-ticket voting was associated with a large increase in roll-off for partisan contests in 2014.

The evidence also indicates that the removal of the straight-ticket voting option produced longer wait times for North Carolina voters in 2014. Following the 2014 election, the North Carolina State Board of Elections conducted a survey of election officials in each North Carolina county to assess the extent of long wait times both during the early voting period and on election day 2014. The survey asked each county board of elections to report the maximum wait time in each county both on election day and during the early voting period – the available categories were less than 30 minutes, 30–60 minutes, and more than 60 minutes. We

TABLE 5.2 *Straight-ticket voting and wait time at the polls, North Carolina, 2014*

Variable	Coefficient (Std. Err.)
Percent African-American	−0.018 (0.011)
Straight-Ticket Average (2010 and 2012)	0.05** (0.02)
Population in Thousands	0.002*** (0.0008)
Cutpoint 1	2.84*** (0.89)
Cutpoint 2	3.68*** (0.91)
N	100
Log-likelihood	−74.04
$\chi^2_{(3)}$	16.07

Note: Cell entries are ordered probit coefficients. Standard errors in parentheses. *** = $p \leq 0.01$; ** = $p \leq 0.05$; * = $p \leq 0.10$.

were able to access and analyze these unique data on wait times from the survey, and in Table 5.2 we use the data on election day wait time to assess the relationship between previous levels of straight-ticket voting in 2010 and 2012 and wait time in 2014. We also control for the population of the county and the percent of the county population that is African-American.

The results in Table 5.2 suggest that counties with larger populations and those with higher levels of straight-ticket voting in previous elections had the highest probability of having long wait times in 2014. The substantive effect for previous levels of straight-ticket voting is quite large. For example, holding all else equal, a county at the 10th percentile of previous straight-ticket voting had a 0.86 probability of having a wait time of less than 30 minutes in 2014 and only a 0.03 probability of having a wait time that exceeded one hour. In contrast, holding all else equal, a county at the 90th percentile of previous straight-ticket voting had a 0.49 probability of a wait time of less than 30 minutes in 2014 and a 0.21 probability of a wait time exceeding one hour. A wait time of more than one hour was seven times more likely in counties that previously had higher levels of straight-ticket voting.

In addition, the Pew Charitable Trust collects data on voter wait time to construct Elections Performance Index. These data are based on interviews conducted with individual voters. In 2014, North Carolina was estimated to have the longest wait time for voting in the country. In 2012, by contrast, twelve states had higher estimated wait times than did North Carolina. Taken together, these data demonstrate that the increased time needed to complete ballots without the straight-ticket voting option likely produced increased wait times for North Carolina voters in 2014, despite the fact that North Carolina had a very short statewide ballot for that election.

5.2.3 North Carolina 2016

In contrast to 2014, the 2016 election in North Carolina included contests for the full council of state in addition to a US Senate contest, the contest for US president, as well as US House and N.C. Senate and House contests. All voters faced a ballot with at least seventeen statewide partisan races in North Carolina in addition to numerous local races. Ballot roll-off was up slightly in statewide partisan races from 5.37 percent in 2012 to 5.71 percent in 2016, but there was considerable variance across the counties. As Figure 5.13 later demonstrates, counties that had higher levels of straight-ticket voting in 2012, the last year it was available, demonstrated the largest increases in roll-off from 2012 to 2016.

An additional potential effect of the elimination of the straight-ticket voting option would be a decline in voter turnout. For voters who wish to vote for all candidates of a single party, the absence of a straight-ticket option increases the amount of time needed to complete the ballot. In North Carolina, a voter who voted a straight ticket in the 2012 election and wished to do the same in 2016 election would have had to make at least sixteen additional marks on the ballot. If no additional polling stations were added, this would inevitably increase the length of lines at polling places during times of high demand for voting. The increased line length would be exacerbated in areas that had experienced high utilization of straight-ticket voting in past elections.

As noted earlier, considerable research has demonstrated that long lines at polling places have a deterrent effect on potential voters. Longer waiting times increase the costs associated with voting and can lead potential voters to forego voting due to inadequate time to stand in long lines.

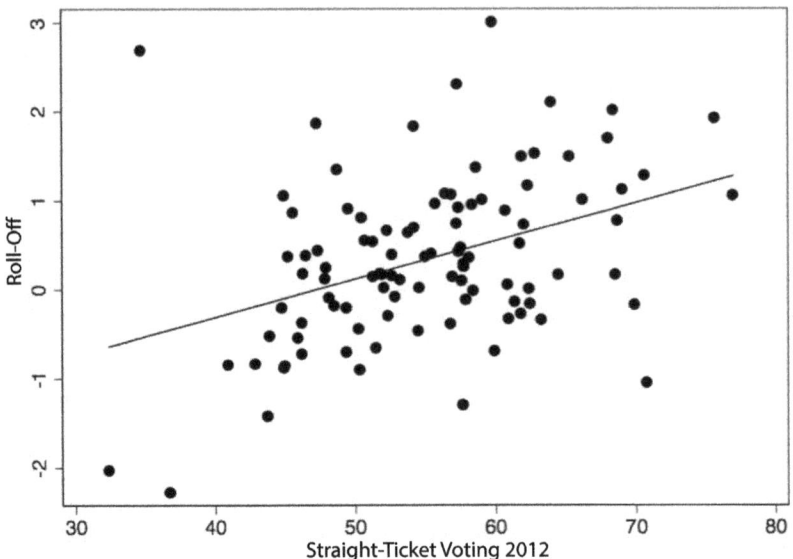

FIGURE 5.13 North Carolina roll-off change, 2012–2016, by straight-ticket voting

Note: Dots represent North Carolina counties; line is a bivariate regression line.

As Figure 5.14 demonstrates, voter turnout in 2016 was down considerably from 2012 levels in North Carolina counties that had high utilization of straight-ticket voting in 2012. These are also counties that have large African-American populations. Turnout among African-American voters was down nationwide in 2016, so it is not necessarily the case that all the decline shown in Figure 5.14 is attributable to the removal of the straight-ticket option.

To more directly assess the relationship between voter turnout in 2016 and previous levels of straight-ticket voting in North Carolina, we utilized the North Carolina voter file and voter history file for registered voters in North Carolina. These two files contain information on whether a registered voter voted, the person's address, and demographic information such as race and gender identity. We combined this information with county-level data on straight-ticket voting in 2012, and the availability of early voting in the county in 2016 to assess factors affecting voter turnout in 2016. We then used these data to fit a logistic regression model of whether an individual voted in the 2016 general election as a function

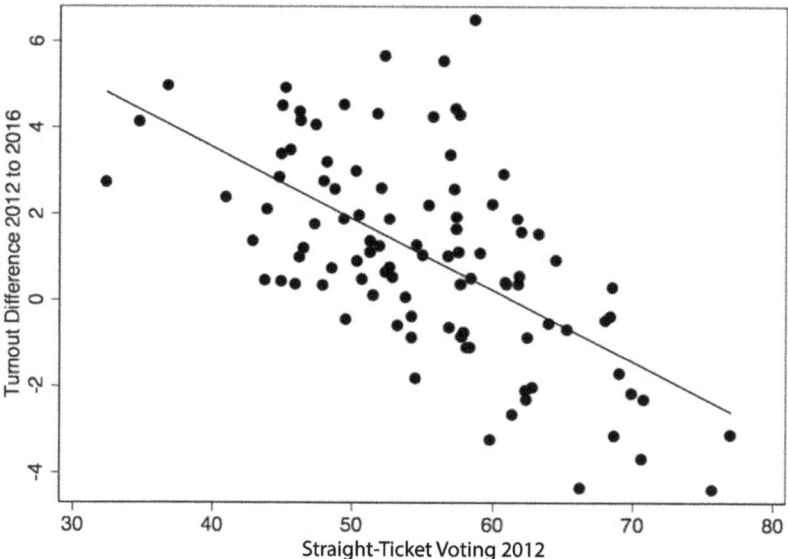

FIGURE 5.14 North Carolina turnout difference, 2012–2016, by straight-ticket voting

Note: Dots represent North Carolina counties; line is a bivariate regression line.

of whether they voted in 2012, their reported race, reported gender, the poverty level of the county, straight-ticket voting level in the county in 2012, and the availability of early voting in the county.

The results, presented in Table 5.3, confirm our expectations and complement our previously reported results. Registered voters who voted in 2012 were more likely to vote in 2016 than were those who did not vote in 2012. Registered voters who reported their race as white and those who identify as female were also more likely to vote than other race and gender categories. Registered voters from counties that provided more early voting opportunities also had higher turnout. Even controlling for these factors, registered voters from counties with higher levels of straight-ticket voting in 2012 were less likely to vote in 2016 than those from counties with lower levels of straight-ticket voting in 2012.

For example, a hypothetical African-American male who voted in 2012 and lives in a county that had the lowest observed level of straight-ticket voting in 2012 had a 0.82 probability of also voting in 2016. However, a hypothetical African-American male who voted in 2012 and

TABLE 5.3 *Straight-ticket elimination and turnout in North Carolina, 2016*

Variable	Coefficient (Std. Err.)
Voted in 2012	2.92*** (0.02)
African American	−0.45*** (0.02)
Native American	−0.48*** (0.02)
Other Ethnicity	−0.50*** (0.05)
Asian American	−0.44*** (0.13)
Multi-Race	−0.94*** (0.05)
Female	0.11*** (0.01)
Early Voting Hours in County	0.08 (0.08)
Straight-Ticket Voting Percentage in 2012	−0.01* (< 0.01)
Intercept	−0.79*** (0.17)
N	5062898
Log-likelihood	−2244310.94
$\chi^2_{(9)}$	72704.98

Note: Data from North Carolina voter file. Cell entries are logit coefficients, standard errors clustered by county in parentheses. $*** = p \leq 0.01$; $** = p \leq 0.05$; $* = p \leq 0.10$.

lives in a county that had the highest observed level of straight-ticket voting in 2012 had a 0.78 probability of also voting in 2016. This 0.04 difference is both statistically and substantively significant. In counties with high levels of straight-ticket voting in 2012, approximately four out of every hundred African-American voters who voted in 2012 were deterred from voting in 2016 due, at least in part, to the elimination of the straight-ticket voting option in North Carolina.

The elimination of straight-ticket voting also reduced the probability of voting for white registered voters. A hypothetical white male who voted in 2012 and lives in a county that had the lowest observed level of straight-ticket voting in 2012 had a 0.88 probability of also voting in 2016. However, a hypothetical white male who voted in 2012 and lives in a county that had the highest observed level of straight-ticket voting in 2012 had a 0.85 probability of also voting in 2016. These results provide powerful evidence that the elimination of straight-ticket voting in North Carolina had a deterrent effect on voter turnout in 2016. The effect was more pronounced in counties that had higher utilization of the straight-ticket voting option in past elections and was more pronounced for African-American voters, who saw their probability of voting in these counties reduced more than for white voters in the same county.

5.2.4 North Carolina Supreme Court, 2016

The removal of the straight-party option in North Carolina also had unintended consequences for the state's Republicans. A seat on the North Carolina Supreme Court was also on the ballot in 2016. The contest was ostensible non-partisan, but informed citizens knew that Mike Morgan was a Democrat while the incumbent Bob Edmunds was a Republican. By law, the candidates were listed alphabetically, with the beginning letter being chosen randomly. In 2016, the letter was "H," which put Morgan first on the ballot line – a position he shared with every Republican on the ballot. Morgan won decisively – by more than 8 points – a result that surprised most political observers, as Republicans won every other statewide judicial race on the ballot. His victory tipped the partisan balance on the North Carolina Supreme Court from majority Republican to majority Democratic.

There are good reasons to suspect that ballot position and the lack of party label had a strong effect on this outcome. There were eighteen statewide contests on the North Carolina ballot in 2016 and for seventeen of those races the correlations between the outcomes at the county level were greater than 0.95, however, the Supreme Court contest correlated with the other statewide races at only 0.72. Clearly, many voters were aware of the candidates' party affiliation. Morgan was endorsed by outgoing president Barack Obama and Morgan ran ads that criticized Edmunds for ruling in favor of Republican designed districting plans. For his part, Edmunds ran ads declaring that he was a "conservative" jurist.

Thus for those paying even cursory attention to the campaign, it would not have been difficult to discern the party affiliation of the candidates.

Despite the partisan affiliations being public, the county-level results suggest that some voters were unaware of this information. In Currituck County, Morgan claimed 57.7 percent of the vote, while the other seventeen Democrats on the statewide ballot averaged only 26.2 percent. Likewise, in Camden County, Morgan claimed 60.5 percent of the vote, while the other seventeen Democrats running statewide averaged only 29.2 percent. What explains these wide disparities? One clear factor is the competitiveness of the counties. The margin of victory for the top vote-getting candidate in the governor's race is positively correlated at 0.61 with the absolute value of the difference between Morgan's vote and that of the Democratic gubernatorial candidate. This suggests a large proportion of voters simply went down the ballot marking the same line – top or bottom – for each statewide race, thus likely erroneously voting for the "wrong" Supreme Court candidate. In addition, some counties reside in media markets that are based outside of North Carolina. The four counties with the largest disparity in vote between the governor's race and the Supreme Court race – Currituck, Clay, Camden, and Cherokee – all are in out of state media markets.[12] Voters residing in these counties likely did not encounter television ads that would have helped them learn the party affiliation of the two candidates. Instead it seems that many habitually marked the name on the first ballot line as they did in every other race.

In Table 5.4 we fit a regression model to try to explain the difference between the gubernatorial vote and the Supreme Court vote in all hundred North Carolina counties. We model this as a function of the margin of victory for the gubernatorial candidate who won each county, an indicator variable for out-of-state media market, the percentage of county residents with college degrees, and the Obama vote in the county in 2012. We include the Obama vote in an effort to see if his endorsement of Morgan helped Morgan more in counties where Obama performed well.

The results suggest that the disparity was wider in counties that were the least competitive at the gubernatorial level in 2016. We also see that the disparity was almost 6 percent greater in counties with out-of-state media markets. At the same time, the disparity was less in counties

---

[12] Currituck and Camden are in the Norfolk, VA, market, Clay is in the Atlanta, GA, market, and Cherokee is in the Chattanooga, TN, market.

TABLE 5.4 *Ballot order and the 2016 North Carolina Supreme Court election*

Variable	Coefficient (Std. Err.)
Governor margin of victory	0.48***
	(0.07)
Out-of-state media market	5.88***
	(1.32)
Percent with college degree	−0.15***
	(0.05)
Obama vote in 2012	−0.30***
	(0.04)
Constant	21.66***
	(2.23)
Number of counties	100
Adjusted R^2	0.69
$F_{(4,95)}$	52.42

Note: Cell entries are linear regression coefficients. Standard errors in parentheses. The dependent variable is the absolute value of the difference between the Democratic vote for Governor and Mike Morgan's vote percentage in a county. *$p \leq .10$; **$p \leq .05$; ***$p \leq .01$

that have more educated voters and in counties that former President Obama performed well in during the 2012 election. Morgan was able to significantly over perform in non-competitive, Republican leaning counties, while holding his own in counties that had a higher proportion of college-educated voters. In the two counties with the highest proportion of college educated residents – Orange and Durham – Morgan got 69.5 percent and 73.11 percent of the vote respectively. He still underperformed Roy Cooper in those counties, but he kept it close enough to prevail statewide.

In the wake of Morgan's victory, the still Republican-controlled General Assembly enacted a bill to make all state judicial elections – including the North Carolina Supreme Court – partisan in an effort to prevent such an outcome in future races. Thus the same majority that enacted the "vote the person, not the party" provision to North Carolina law in 2013 had come full circle by 2016. They apparently decided that they wanted to make it more likely that voters would vote the party not the person for state Supreme Court elections post-2016.[13]

5.3 COMPARING MICHIGAN AND NORTH CAROLINA

While we think our results for North Carolina are persuasive, the fact the judicial ruling enjoined the removal of the straight-ticket voting option for Michigan in 2016 gives us a unique opportunity to directly assess the effect of straight-ticket removal on ballot roll-off in these two states. Both legislatures (Michigan and North Carolina) intended to remove the straight ticket voting option for its voters, but Michigan was unable to carry out the removal of straight-ticket voting due to a court ruling. The court ruling was exogenous to the political process that enacted the statute removing the straight-ticket option so it creates analytical leverage for identifying a causal effect. North Carolina's voters received the treatment of having the straight-ticket option removed, while Michigan's voters in essence served as the control group. Both legislatures intended to treat their voters, but Michigan's voters did not receive the treatment due to a legal intervention that operates independently of the political process that ordered the treatment.

---

[13] The postscript to this story involves the 2018 contest for a seat on the North Carolina Supreme Court. A Republican incumbent, Barbara Jackson, was seeking reelection to the seat. The Republican majority in the General Assembly tried a usual tactic to keep this seat. In addition to making the contest explicitly partisan, they decided to forego a primary election. Thus, all candidates seeking the seat would be listed on the general election ballot. Apparently, the thought was that no Republican would challenge Jackson while the Democrats would likely have more than one candidate for the seat and would likely split the Democratic vote among two or more candidates. However, only one Democrat, Anita Earls, chose to seek the seat, while an additional Republican, Chris Anglin, also sought the seat. This set up a general election with two Republicans and one Democrat – exactly the opposite outcome of what the state Republican party hoped for. In a last-ditch effort to save the seat, the General Assembly enacted a law that would have retroactively removed Anglin from the ballot by creating a requirement that a person must have affiliated with a given party more than ninety days before they filed for the seat. This ninety-day requirement had been removed by the Republican-controlled General Assembly the year before. Anglin had changed his party affiliation inside the ninety-day window, but he successfully sued to prevent the law being implemented for the 2018 election. Earls subsequently won the seat with 49.56 percent of the vote as Jackson and Anglin split the majority of voters who supported a Republican in the contest. Despite the constant effort of the Republican majority in the General Assembly to induce a Republican majority on the North Carolina Supreme Court, they currently only hold one seat to six for the Democratic Party.

Given that one set of voters received the treatment (straight-ticket removal) and one did not, it is possible to directly assess the effects of straight-ticket removal by comparing the results from Michigan and North Carolina in 2016. To do this we employed a statistical procedure known as Coarsened Exact Matching (CEM) (Iacus et al. 2012). The CEM routine allowed us to identify counties in Michigan and North Carolina that had high similarity on political and socioeconomic factors such as the poverty rate, the percentage of African-American citizens, the county's vote for President Obama in 2012, and the voter turnout rate in 2012. Similar counties are preserved for analysis while counties in each state that do not provide a close match with a county in the comparison state are omitted.[14]

Once the matched counties were identified, the effect of the treatment, in this case STV removal, was estimated via linear regression. We estimate the effect of straight-ticket removal on the statewide change in partisan roll-off rate from 2012 to 2016 with positive numbers indicating more roll-off in 2016 than in 2012. Independent variables include the four variables used to match counties and an indicator variable set equal to one for Michigan counties. The results presented in Figure 5.15 demonstrate that the average roll-off rate was approximately 2.2 percent lower in Michigan counties than in North Carolina counties in 2016. In North Carolina this equates to approximately 115,000 fewer ballots being completed than would have been this case had the straight-ticket option been in place. This is a non-trivial effect, as seven statewide offices in North Carolina were decided by fewer than 115,000 votes in 2016, including the governorship. Similarly, our results suggest that in Michigan, implementation of a straight-ticket voting ban for 2016 would have likely produced a 2.2 percent decrease in ballot roll-off which also equates to approximately 115,000 votes. Again, this is non-trivial effect as statewide contests in Michigan are regularly decided by margins smaller than this. Examples include the governing bodies of all three state universities in 2016.

The cases of Michigan and North Carolina are illustrative of the key themes of this book. In both cases there are partisan majorities who had

---

[14] North Carolina has 100 counties and Michigan has 83. For the CEM analysis, 106 total counties (34 from North Carolina and 72 from Michigan) were retained for analysis. North Carolina has a much larger number of counties with a substantial African-American population (median is 18.3 percent) than does Michigan (median is 1.2 percent) so a smaller proportion of North Carolina counties were retained for the CEM analysis.

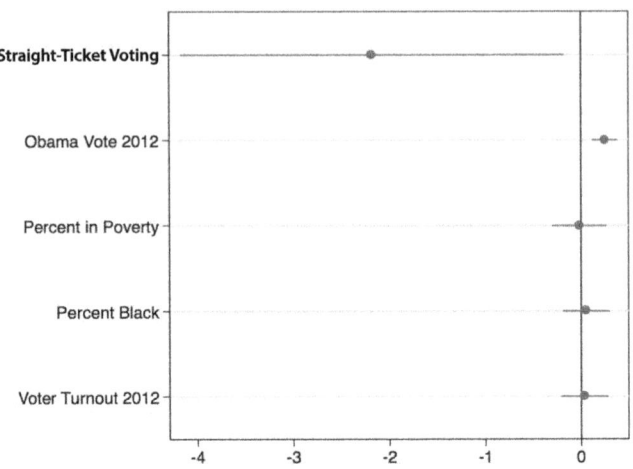

FIGURE 5.15 Effect of straight-ticket voting ban on change in roll-off, 2012–2016

Note: Estimates from a post-matching linear regression. Dots represent linear regression coefficients, bars are 95 percent confidence intervals.

reason to believe that their hold on power was tenuous and in both cases they undertook ballot reform measures that would help tighten their hold on power. Our results, especially in North Carolina, demonstrate that removing the straight-ticket option increased ballot roll-off, increased line length at polling places, and contributed to a decline in turnout in areas and among voters most likely to vote for the Democratic party. Michigan and North Carolina are both relatively large states with a mix of rural and urban areas and relatively large minority population. In the next section, we consider the cases of Iowa and West Virginia to see how the effects of ballot design changes play out in more rural, white, and less-densely populated states.

5.4 IOWA AND WEST VIRGINIA

5.4.1 Iowa

The Iowa legislature initially adopted the party column with box ballot format in 1892, and they used the party column without box from 1906 to 1918. The party column with box was readopted in 1918 and remained in place through the 1996 election. From 1996 to 2016, Iowa employed the office bloc ballot with the party box option. The party box was eliminated in 2017 as part of a comprehensive election reform package that shortened the early voting period in Iowa, and instituted a voter identification requirement for Iowa voters. This bill was passed with an overwhelming percentage of Republicans voting in favor and most Democrats opposing the change and was signed into law by a Republican Governor.

As is true in other states for which we have data, straight-ticket voting was quite popular in Iowa.[15] Approximately 35 percent of Iowa voters used the straight-ticket option in 2014, but usage varied widely across counties. Only 15.2 percent of voters in Sioux County chose to use the straight-ticket option in 2014, compared to 74.9 percent in Osceola County. Unlike in other states we analyzed, for Iowa's 2014 election we see no clear pattern between the prevalence of straight-ticket voting and roll-off in down-ballot races. This is somewhat surprising given that the 2014 election had numerous statewide offices on the ballot in Iowa.

For 2016, Iowa voters were presented with a much shorter ballot. Approximately 30 percent of voters used the straight-ticket option, with the variation in usage ranging from 15 percent to just over 40 percent. The only statewide, partisan races were for US president, US Senate, and US House, so the opportunities for roll-off were fewer than was the case in 2014. However, we do see a familiar pattern with respect to straight-ticket voting and roll-off. As Figure 5.16 demonstrates, counties with higher levels of straight-ticket voting had much lower levels of roll-off from president to the US House.

The 2018 election was the first time in a century that Iowa voters had gone to the polls without having the option of voting a straight-party ticket. Iowa Democrats were worried that their fortunes would suffer due to the removal of the straight ticket. They feared that the President Trump's low approval ratings would drive a large number of voters to the polls who would be stymied by long lines and a confusing ballot structure. One party official thought that new voters, in particular, could struggle without the straight-ticket option noting that, "When you come in to vote, you have a large ballot. . . . The long line of people in our office,

---

[15] We thank Wes Hicok from the Iowa Secretary of State's office for his help compiling straight-ticket data for Iowa.

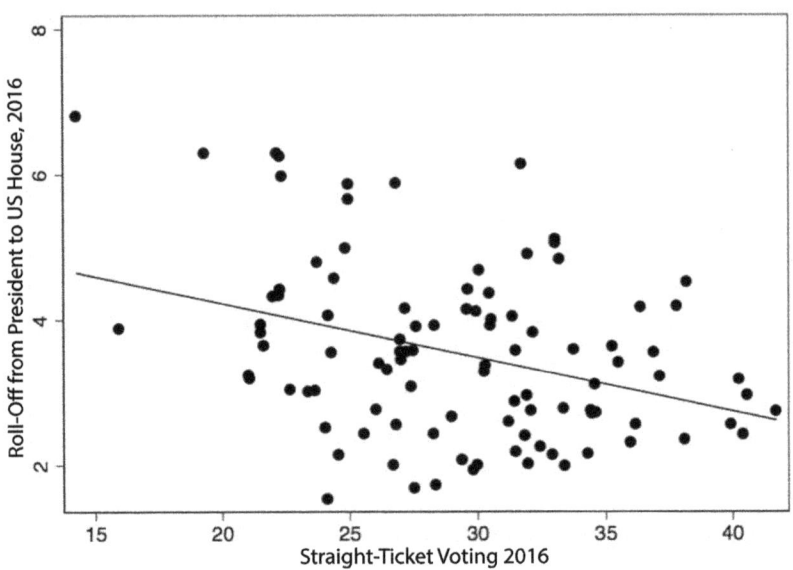

FIGURE 5.16 Straight-ticket voting and ballot roll-off, Iowa, 2016

Note: Dots represent Iowa counties; line is a bivariate regression line.

they seem anxious. I think it's just a lot of people were party loyalists on both sides who were used to just filling in one circle."[16]

There appeared to be good reasons for Iowa Democrats to be anxious about this change in voting procedure. Straight-ticket voting was quite common in Iowa counties that had both large populations and high levels of support for Democratic candidates. However, we have found no evidence to suggest that the removal of the straight-ticket voting option harmed Iowa Democrats in statewide or federal races in 2018. To the extent that there is a relationship between previous levels of straight-ticket voting and roll-off, it is negative, but these differences are not statistically or substantively significant. We did not analyze local-level races, so it is entirely possible that roll-off increased in those races. We also note that the 2018 election cycle featured an unusually engaged and motivated Democratic electorate due to the low approval ratings of President Donald Trump, so it could be that the particulars of the

[16] Korecki, Natasha. "Iowa Democrats Fume over GOP Change to Ballot Law." Politico, 23 Oct. 2018. https://www.politico.com/story/2018/10/23/iowa-voting-law-midterm-elections-929530

2018 election cycle muted the effects of institutional change, but more elections will have to occur before we can assess this relationship.[17]

5.4.2 West Virginia

West Virginia adopted the party column with box format in 1891. This ballot format stayed in place for more than a century until West Virginia changed to the office bloc with party box ballot format prior to the 1994 election, and it remained in place through the 2014 election. Like Iowa, West Virginia's straight-ticket elimination was pushed by the Republican majorities in each chamber. The final passage votes received support from all West Virginia Republicans and divided the Democrats. The Democratic leadership was opposed to the bill with Senator Mike Romano arguing that the ban on straight-ticket voting would discourage people from voting.

Unfortunately, we have limited straight-ticket voting data from West Virginia. We have information on straight-ticket voting for the 2010 and 2014 elections in West Virginia, but we were unable to obtain straight-ticket results for the 2012 election.[18] West Virginia conducts most of its elections for statewide office during presidential years, so our data for 2010 and 2014 are for years with relatively short ballots. We do have results for the US House and US Senate for comparable elections before and after the elimination of the straight-ticket option, which allows us to draw some inferences about the relationship between straight-ticket voting and roll-off.

Despite limited data availability, the patterns in West Virginia are very similar to what we have seen in other states. As Figure 5.17 demonstrates, before the elimination of the straight-ticket option, roll-off from the US Senate race to the US House race was much lower in counties that had higher levels of straight-ticket voting. As was true in Michigan and North Carolina, counties with higher proportions of non-white residents had higher levels of straight-ticket voting. These counties also typically are higher performing areas for Democrats.

---

[17] In addition, Iowa has very few cites with more than 100,000 residents (it has three, compared to nine in North Carolina) and has very few African-American voters (<5.0 percent). It could be that the effects of it taking longer to complete the ballot are muted in a state like Iowa that likely has very little crowding at polling places due to its low population density.

[18] In stark contrast to Iowa, the West Virginia Secretary of State's office was entirely unhelpful and borderline hostile to our inquiries about obtaining additional data.

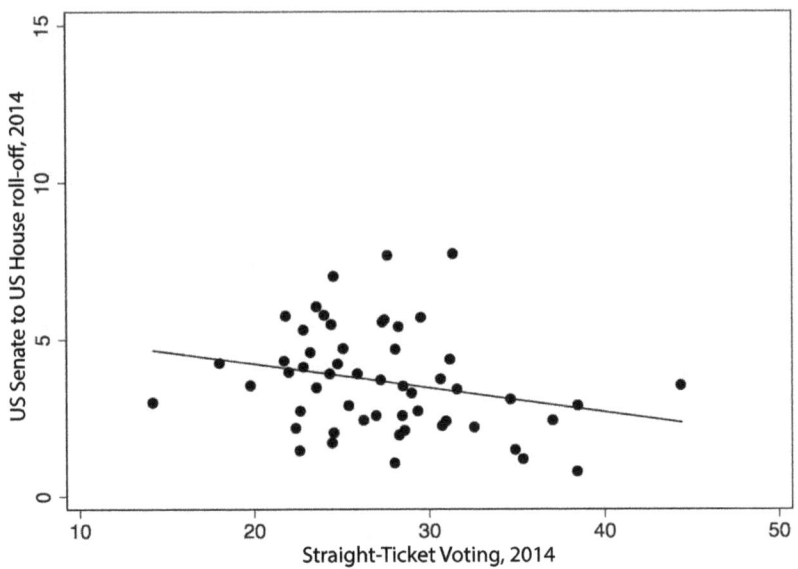

FIGURE 5.17 Straight-ticket voting and roll-off, West Virginia, 2014

Note: Dots represent West Virginia counties; line is a bivariate regression line.

In Figure 5.18, we plot roll-off from the US Senate to US House against the 2014 level of straight-ticket voting. In doing so, we see an inversion of the pattern from 2014. In 2014, areas with high levels of straight-ticket voting had lower levels of roll-off, but in 2018, it was counties that previously had higher levels of straight-ticket voting that had the highest levels of roll-off from the US Senate race to the US House race. Thus the change in voting procedure is clearly associated with an increase in ballot roll-off in areas where the straight-ticket option was popular.

As we noted earlier, we lack data on the extent of straight-ticket voting in 2012 or any other presidential year. We did compare roll-off rates from the presidential election to the US House for 2012, which was the last presidential year election with straight-ticket voting, to those from 2016, the first election with the straight-ticket option to see what patterns emerged. Overall, the roll-off rates across the two years were identical statewide at 4.59 percent. However, if we compare the difference in roll-off rates in the same county to the average level of straight-ticket voting in 2010 and 2014 (as the best proxy for 2012), we do see a relationship

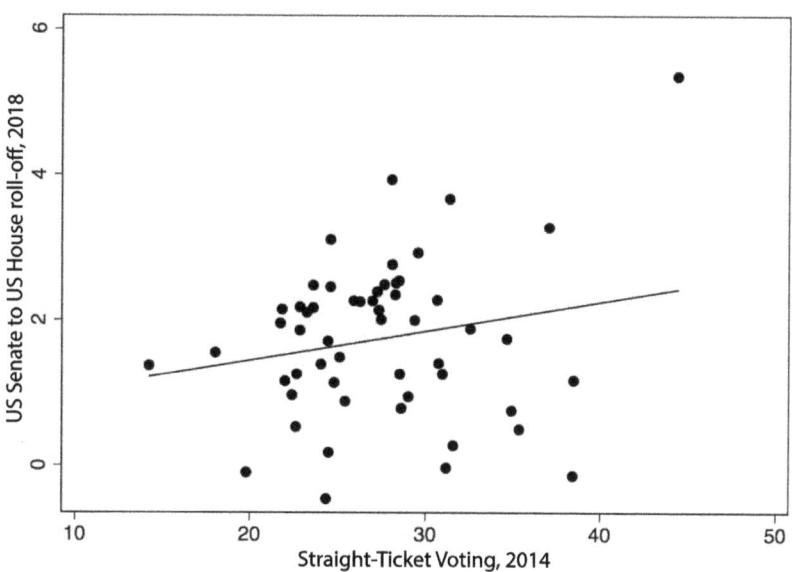

FIGURE 5.18 Straight-ticket voting and roll-off, West Virginia, 2018

Note: Dots represent West Virginia counties; line is a bivariate regression line.

between previous levels of straight-ticket voting and roll-off. As Figure 5.19 demonstrates, counties that had higher levels of straight-ticket voting in 2010 and 2014 had the greatest increase in roll-off from 2012 to 2016. This again suggests that the removal of the straight-ticket option in West Virginia is associated with lower levels of ballot completion in areas where voters were most likely to choose the straight-ticket option. Given the racial and political characteristics of the counties that had high levels of straight-ticket usage, this change in voting procedure may have produced fewer votes for Democrats in down-ballot races.

5.5 CONCLUSION

This chapter demonstrates that the politics of ballot law choices are as contested and consequential as ever. As we noted earlier, the current political climate in many ways mimics the Progressive Era we analyze in Chapter 3. The political parties are starkly divided over most items on the policy agenda and the competition for majority control both in state legislatures and the US Congress is fierce. Partisan control of the US

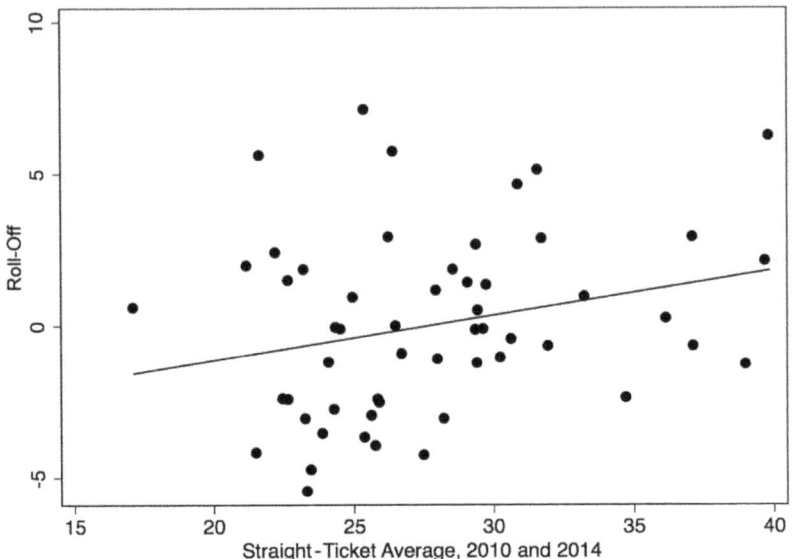

FIGURE 5.19 West Virginia roll-off change, 2012–2016

Note: Dots represent West Virginia counties; line is a bivariate regression line.

House has changed hands in three of past seven elections. In this environment, strategic politicians have latched on to any available strategy to gain or maintain a partisan advantage, including manipulation of state ballot laws.

Our analysis demonstrates that these changes have largely been effective. The data we analyze here suggests that removal of the straight-ticket option in some states is associated with a decline in ballot completion rates in many states. Our individual-level analysis of North Carolina demonstrates that straight-ticket removal not only produced lower levels of ballot completion, but it is also associated with a demonstrable decline in voter turnout. The changes we analyze have uniformly been implemented by Republican-led state legislatures. As our detailed analysis of Michigan indicates, the partisan actors seem to understand the effects that these changes will have and they pursue them vigorously.

Given the evidence that these changes work and the continued intense partisan competition, we expect politicians to continue to pursue them in the future. Our results on Iowa suggest that the effect may be muted in states that are more white and rural, but we do not have enough data from the contemporary era to assess that potential relationship systematically. Texas, a large, urban state with a significant and growing minority population, has passed legislation that would eliminate the straight-ticket option beginning with the 2020 general election. Given the demographics of the state and the fact that it has a fast-growing population, we would expect the consequences of this change to be immense in Texas. A similar change was enacted in Pennsylvania and will likely have a large effect there as well, especially in Philadelphia and Pittsburgh.

6

Reconsidering the American Ballot

This book has provided an examination of more than a century's worth of changes in ballot design in the American states. Our analyses have found that ballot design has had important consequences for almost all aspects of electoral politics. Throughout this history, we have encountered politicians routinely fighting over ballot design in the quest for personal and partisan gain. The ferocity of these clashes has varied over time, with vitriolic fights defining the early twentieth century, followed by relative calm in the late twentieth century. Recent events in Michigan and North Carolina demonstrate that quarrels over ballot architecture have regained steam in the early decades of the twenty-first century. Over the past twenty years a number of states have removed the straight-ticket provision from their ballots. In many cases, intense controversy surrounded these changes. These fights have embroiled a number of state legislatures, produced numerous legal showdowns, and in one case resulted in voters overturning the decisions of their state legislature. In this concluding chapter, we summarize our findings and then discuss implications of our work for both academic scholarship and the future of voting in America.

6.1 THE CONSEQUENCES OF BALLOT DESIGN

A key feature of ballot design is the default option. As Thaler and Sunstein (2008) argue, humans are prone to following the path of least resistance. Simply put, people are predisposed to follow the default, or easiest, option presented by the choice architecture. The canonical example is employer-provided retirement savings plans. More workers participate if they have to opt out of the plan than if they have to opt in to the plan, despite the fact that this decision often has immense financial consequences for the worker. The decision to vote or not and how to fill out a particular ballot will rarely, if ever, be as consequential for an individual as their choices over retirement savings. Thus it should not be surprising that our analyses in this book consistently demonstrated that ballot design differences affect how voters make ballot choices.

In the context of ballot design, the path of least resistance for many voters is to simply vote a straight ticket. For example, as we detail in Chapter 4, for much of the twentieth century Connecticut required voters to first pull a straight-party lever before making any other ballot choices. They could then proceed to "cut" as many of these options as they wished by moving individual levers, but the default was a straight-ticket vote for all partisan offices on the ballot. With this ballot design in place, straight-ticket voting was common and ballot roll-off was minuscule (less than 1 percent). However, once the default option was changed, ballot roll-off increased sharply. While this case is extreme, we found more generally that the party column ballot, as well as the straight-ticket provision, greases the wheels for voters who are inclined to cast a straight ticket. It also creates the default of voters casting a vote for all the offices on the ballot. By contrast, the office bloc ballot flips the default setting. Now voters have to work their way through the ballot making office-by-office choices along the way. As we have found throughout this book, the consequences of these simple nudges can be far-reaching. The office bloc format leads to more ballot roll-off, more split-ticket voting, and enhances the electoral advantages accruing to incumbents.

Second, ballot architecture can directly influence how voters manage the complex choices they face. The party column ballot with the straight-ticket provision simplifies complex decisions. A voter can boil their decisions over which candidate to choose for each office down to one decision – vote for the Democratic or Republican slate – that can induce some voters to choose to vote a straight ticket. As we saw in Chapter 5, Michigan Republicans complained that the dominance of the straight-ticket option made it difficult for them to run vigorous campaigns for down ballot offices. Even without the straight-ticket option, the alignment of choices in the party column ballot into one column visually frames the choice for the voter. By contrast, the office bloc ballot requires voters to make decisions office-by-office. To be sure, a voter can still use the simple cue of just voting for candidates of their preferred party, but the architecture of the office bloc nudges voters, on the margin, toward splitting their ticket for the occasional office. It also nudges voters toward not completing their ballot, leading to down ballot roll-off.

As we have found, these nudges add up to produce substantial collective outcomes. Consider the case of waiting times at polling stations. Ballots that take longer to fill out, such as the office bloc ballot, lead voters to spend more time in the voting booth. This, inevitably, produces longer lines at polling stations, which increases the costs of voting for potential voters. For example, wait times in North Carolina increased substantially after the straight-ticket option was removed from the ballot. The resulting longer lines then led to some potential voters giving up and going home, rather than waiting to vote (Spencer and Markovits 2010). Moreover, these down-stream consequences do not fall equally across the electorate. In our analysis of North Carolina, we found that minority voters were most affected by the switch in ballot formats and the resulting increase in waiting times. This is consistent with the voter turnout literature, which finds that whiter, richer, more educated voters are more likely to be able to bear the costs of voting (Rosenstone and Hansen 1993).

Third, ballot architecture can help, or hinder, the ability of voters to make choices that enhance their welfare. This is especially true for less informed or sophisticated voters. As we have found, ballot nudges can be most pronounced among less educated voters. One dramatic example comes from the early twentieth century in Maryland, where the state's Democrats implemented a ballot type explicitly designed to make it difficult, if not impossible, for African Americans and immigrants to complete the ballot correctly. In this period in which literacy rates were not nearly as high as today, ballot architecture could have an immense effect on illiterate voters. The presence of distinct party emblems, for example, at the top of the ballot-aided voters who had difficulty reading the names of candidates or political parties. The visual cues assisted these voters in making decisions that enhanced their personal welfare – voting for their preferred candidates and that had the effect of excluding a portion of the electorate from participating in elections.

6.2 THE CAUSES OF BALLOT DESIGN

Given the importance of ballot design for electoral outcomes, we directed our attention to better understanding ballot architects and their motivations. In the United States, this has primarily been politicians in state legislatures. The strategic problems these politicians face have varied considerably across states and across time. As conditions change nationally, state politicians have used ballot architecture as a tool of adaptation. During periods of intense, nationalized competition, there is a heightened incentive to manipulate electoral laws – including ballot formats – to gain a partisan advantage.

With the prize of national government in reach, both parties have a greater incentive to grasp for every extra advantage possible (Lee 2016). Moreover, greater partisan voting leads to greater predictability about how changes in voting architecture will translate into outcomes. When voters are more likely to vote a straight ticket, parties can make more accurate forecasts about the consequences of changing ballot formats. For parties that want to catch presidential coattails and minimize down ballot roll-off, the party column and/or straight-ticket provision becomes attractive. Likewise, a party wishing to insulate itself from coattails, we have found, would prefer an office bloc ballot without a straight-ticket option. But this decision becomes important because voters have such strong partisan behavior. Parties can more easily predict the outcomes of institutional manipulation when voters behave in consistent and predictable manner. When voters are more behaviorally inclined to cross-party lines, the effects of manipulation of ballot formats becomes more difficult to forecast.

We explored this argument by analyzing the design of electoral architecture in three different historical periods. The first era we explored was the late nineteenth and early twentieth century. During this period, ballot architecture became a weapon in a larger war being fought on two fronts. The first front was fought along standard party lines between Democrats and Republicans. The close competition between Democrats and Republicans in the late nineteenth and early twentieth century fostered numerous attempts to rework ballots for partisan gain. The case studies of Maryland, California, and New York that we provided in Chapter 3 all testify to the intense partisan battles over ballot design that took place in the state legislatures.

The second front was between reformers and the old-guard party machines. What makes this earlier era especially interesting was that the battles over ballot architecture also took place within the parties. In California, for example, the Republicans broke into factional warfare over ballot design. The reform-oriented Progressive Republicans, led by figures such as Hiram Johnson, sought to nudge voters away from straight-ticket voting behavior. In doing so, these reformers sought to undercut the voting foundation of party machine strength. In contrast, the old-guard Republican operatives used ballot design in their rearguard action to fight off progressive reformers. By insisting on the use of the party circle on the ballot, they attempted to nudge voters in a strictly partisan direction.

As the twentieth century moved on, the nature of party competition changed, and the strategic problems that parties needed to address changed with it. Whereas the late nineteenth and early twentieth century featured a high degree of polarized, straight-ticket voting, the middle of the twentieth century featured greater split-ticket voting. A less partisan electorate changed the incentives for strategic politicians. The problem was less about trying to beat the other side and more about protecting incumbents against electoral downturns. This expectation matches the pattern found in the middle of the twentieth century, which we call the "Personal Vote Era." During this period of heightened split-ticket voting, the frequency of ballot format changes dissipated. The changes that did happen elicited much less controversy compared to the early twentieth century or the more recent twenty-first century, but that did not lessen the consequences. As we demonstrated in Chapter 4, ballot changes made during this era contributed to the growth of the incumbency advantage and altered the way that some members behaved in Congress.

Since the early 2000s, fights over ballot design have become considerably more contentious in state legislatures. The rise of partisan polarization, nationalized elections, and close party competition in Washington, DC, fueled a concomitant rise in fights over ballot architecture. The strategic problem facing politicians today is once again how to win elections in a world with few persuadable voters. The high levels of partisan voting mean that politicians must find other paths to victory beyond persuasion. Ballot architecture provides one avenue. In just the last decade alone, a number of state legislatures have modified their ballots – usually removing the straight-ticket option – with the goal of nudging the electorate in their preferred direction. In North Carolina and Michigan, for example, Republicans removed the straight-ticket option to nudge Democratic voters, many of whom were African-American, away from voting a Democratic straight-ticket or from voting at all. The controversy surrounding these actions, and the continuance of partisan polarization into the future, suggests that partisan clashes over ballot architecture will continue for the foreseeable future.

6.3 SCHOLARLY IMPLICATIONS

Beyond helping scholars better understand American electoral development, the findings in this book raise important implications for at least four research debates about democratic elections.

First, one of the long-running debates in the study of democratic politics concerns the levels of information voters need to adequately participate in an election. A truism of survey research is that the typical voter knows few, if any, details about the issue positions of candidates or parties (Converse 1964). One school of thought charges that a poorly informed electorate undermines the very foundations of democratic theory. Achen and Bartels (2017), for instance, have recently argued that the logical endpoint of voter ignorance is partisan tribalism. A competing school of thought points to informational shortcuts as a way for voters to fill the informational void (Lupia and McCubbins 1998; Sniderman 2017). Notably, party labels figure prominently in this school of thought. Party labels are inexpensive and simple pieces of information that voters can use to make reasonable decisions. One need not be well-versed on the particular issue stances of each candidate. Knowing simply that a candidate is a Democrat or a Republican provides a great deal of information to voters. In this way, party labels serve as one solution to the strategic information problem faced by voters and the candidates who want to persuade them.

Ballot architecture is an essential, but often ignored, structural aspect of this debate. Scholars involved in this debate have seemingly forgotten the findings of Campbell and Miller (1957, 299) who helpfully point out that, "Any attempt to explain why the voter marks a straight or split ballot must take account of the physical characteristics of the election ballot." In the United States, not all voters face the same decision-making framework. By directing voters to focus on parties not people, the party column and straight-ticket provision can help solve the problem of rational ignorance for voters. On the other hand, by simplifying choices the party column may encourage voters to become even less informed. It may encourage voters to make choices for offices and candidates for which they know nothing about. Or they may abstain instead of casting a vote for a candidate for which they have no information. Taking into account ballot structure, we argue, is a much-needed addition to scholarly understanding of how voters make decisions.

Second, another longstanding debate among political scientists concerns the role of parties in democratic politics. One school of thought holds that parties serve as the building blocks of politics in the United States, with partisan attachments serving as the primary factor behind both electoral and legislative behavior (Cox and McCubbins 1993, 2005; Rohde 1991). Another school of thought suggests politicians in the United States cater to the parochial interests of their districts, even if this runs contrary to the collective interests of their political party (Mayhew 1974).

In this book, we have found that ballot architecture dramatically shifts the emphasis voters put on parties versus candidates. For those desiring responsible political parties, then the party column and/or straight-ticket provision would seem a better design option. The party column, or straight-ticket provision, nudges voters to vote in a partisan manner. As a result, politicians elected under a party column or straight-ticket ballot have less incentive to carve out personal electoral niches. They are more likely to work together as a party team, both in voting and in electioneering.

By contrast, office bloc politicians display a greater willingness to traffic in the politics of public opinion. For instance, we found that House members from office bloc districts introduced substantially more legislation than those from party column districts. Likewise, office bloc representatives are more sensitive to public sentiment in their districts.

Third, a vast literature in congressional and state elections examines the causes and consequences of the electoral advantages held by incumbents. Indeed, one can frame much of the last forty years of scholarship in US congressional elections as a quest to determine why incumbents so routinely outperform their opponents. The literature has pointed to a number of explanations, ranging from gerrymandering to the resources of holding office to campaign finance to the strategic decisions of candidates. We do not deny that any, or all, of these factors, may be at play. What we have found, however, is that ballot formats produced considerable variation across districts in the size of the incumbency advantage. In short, future theoretical and empirical work on legislative elections should take ballot formats into greater consideration.

Fourth, and finally, the findings presented in this book offer a reminder that party competition extends well beyond ideological competition. The dominant scholarly model of party competition views elections primarily as an ideological competition. Parties craft issue platforms for the purpose of persuading the median voter and thereby winning office (Downs 1957). Building on the ideas found in Downs, an enormous literature developed to explore the dynamics of spatial competition and the issue positions parties employ to persuade voters. Following this line of research, academic studies of democratic elections, past and present, often focus on the grand battles between political ideologies. In the context of US political history the various ideological struggles across, and within, parties include slavery, economic development, foreign policy, civil rights, immigration, and the scope of government. To be sure ideological conflict is an essential filament of democracy.

But this ideological competition is often assumed to take place against a stable institutional background. As scholars like William Riker pointed out, politicians do not always take the rules of the game as they find it. The rules are themselves often the subject of political contestation. Following these insights, political scientists and legal academics have paid close attention to voter identification laws, gerrymandering, and campaign finance, among others. To be sure these demand attention. But ballot design needs to be accorded a higher place in academic research on electoral manipulation as well.

6.4 POLICY IMPLICATIONS: DESIGNING A BETTER BALLOT

The analysis of this book also raises important implications for the practice of American elections. In particular, it raises the normative consideration of where in the political system ballot design decisions should reside and who should make those decisions. In the United States, the administration of elections is left primarily to state and local governments. Although the federal government has standardized a number of election rules, the states continue to retain a great deal of authority over election law. State governments are responsible for a host of electoral rules including drawing district boundaries, registration requirements, nomination procedures, filing fees, and numerous other aspects of elections. Over time, the federal government has intervened to regulate and standardize some aspects of elections. The creation of a standardized day for federal elections, for example, came about in the 1870s. National standards for the protection of voting rights occurred in the 1960s. However, most design and implementation decisions remain with state and local governments.

The decentralization of election law in the United States thus opens the door to manipulation by state and local politicians. The driving goal of a political party is to win elections. Parties, and their candidates, almost always espouse their vision of the good society. But these proposed ideologies have long been understood to be a means to an end – capturing governmental power (e.g., Downs 1957). Parties are, first and foremost, comprised of self-interested actors who want to capture political power (Aldrich 1995). Exploiting electoral institutions, with the aim of influencing down-stream outcomes, provides a key tool in the quest for electoral victory. The manipulation of electoral rules can take a number of different forms. These rules determine who votes, when they vote, how they vote, and how those votes get translated into offices. Throughout American history, altering the scope of the electorate has been one primary vehicle. Sometimes this can be a force toward expanding the electorate. But many other times it has been a force for voter suppression.

One can point to the centuries-long suppression of African American voting rights as Exhibit A in the case against electoral federalism. Even after the abolition of slavery, and the passage of the 13th, 14th, and 15th Amendments, the right of African Americans to vote was at the mercy of state and local politicians. From the imposition of Jim Crow laws in the late nineteenth century until the civil rights victories of the 1960s, African Americans were forcefully denied the right to vote throughout most of the US South and in other parts of the country. State laws passed in the late nineteenth and early twentieth century – literacy tests, poll taxes, and so forth – effectively eliminated African American voting in the South (Kousser 1974). Only with the intervention of the federal government following the 1964 Civil Rights Act and the 1965 Voting Rights Act did the suppression of African American voting begin to dissipate.

But even today, as we have found in this book, leaving these issues to the states jeopardizes those hard-fought historical victories. Notably the US Supreme Court decision in *Shelby County* v. *Holder* (2013) overturned Section 4(b) of the Voting Rights Act (VRA). This section of the VRA provided the formula that determined which jurisdictions were subject to the pre-clearance requirement. Jurisdictions subject to "pre-clearance" were required to receive approval from the Justice Department before making changes to their election laws. Hence, by overturning Section 4(b), the Supreme Court in effect gutted the preclearance requirement altogether.

A number of state legislatures quickly exploited the lifting of preclearance. As we saw in Chapters 1 and 5, perhaps the most notorious recent instance happened in North Carolina. Shortly after the Shelby County decision, Republicans in North Carolina passed a law imposing a voter identification requirement, eliminated same-day registration during the early voting period, and eliminated out-of-precinct voting. In addition, they removed the straight-ticket provision of the ballot. The actions of North Carolina were mirrored in a number of other states that had been previously subject to VRA preclearance. Many aspects of this law were later struck down by a federal court, but the battle over voting rights in North Carolina continues to this day.

The history of African American voter suppression by states alone could be considered reason enough to question the utility of letting states administer the architecture of American elections. Of course, the question is whether the benefits of electoral federalism outweigh the costs?

One advantage of a decentralized voting system that relies on myriad types of ballots, machines, and databases is that it is more difficult for a single equipment failure to affect multiple jurisdictions. The decentralized system that we have in the United States, while clearly not impervious to attacks by those with bad intentions, is more resistant to tampering because of the multitude of disconnected systems in use.

Additionally, as is true with other public policy issues, one potential virtue of federalism is that it allows states to experiment. Sometimes this experimentation has been a force driving the expansion of voting rights. To take one notable historical example, the expansion of female suffrage started in the states. More recently, a number of states have been in the vanguard of making it easier to register. California, for example, passed a law automatically providing voter registration upon receiving a driver's license. A person could opt out if they wanted. However, in the language of behavioral economics, the new rule changed the default. By changing the default action – that is, a person is automatically registered unless one opts out – the state incorporates many new voters into the electorate. Other states have followed including Oregon. Similarly, states such as Oregon and Colorado have experienced with voting by mail as the primary means of voting rather than relying on staffing scores of precincts throughout states and localities.

Of course, one might respond that the passage of automatic voter registration in California was no less politically motivated than the imposition of voter-ID laws or the banning of straight-ticket voting in other states. The pool of new potential voters very likely tilts toward the Democratic Party. As some indication of the partisan ramifications, the law was passed by strong Democratic majorities in the legislature and opposed by Republicans. Nevertheless, laws like the California automatic registration are expansionary rather than restrictive. We would argue that the fact the modern-day Democrats prefer laws that expand the electorate and make it easier to vote while Republicans prefer a smaller electorate and more barriers to voting is in no way a principled position held by either party. History suggests the parties would reverse their respective positions if they found it politically expedient to do so. It just so happens that at this moment in history, normatively appealing expansionary voting laws happen to be in the best interests of the Democratic Party.

However, to the extent one thinks democracy should value expansionary, rather than restrictive, voting laws, there may be some value in state experimentation as it helps scholars and politicians understand what types of institutions do and do not expand the participation rate among eligible voters. For example, Burden et al. (2014) demonstrate that increasing the number of days that individuals can vote via early voting does not necessarily boost turnout. A key question though is how we weigh the benefits of continued experimentation with the harms done by parties enacting electoral regimes that work to entrench power by shaping the electorate?

In our view, the evidence in support of national standards for ballot design and other aspects of election administration far outweigh the costs. The continuing efforts by certain states to suppress the votes of racial minorities, the young, and other groups is morally and legally suspect. While neither of us purports to be a scholar of constitutional law, we also think that allowing states to shape the voting process in ways that benefit the party in power potentially raises equal protection and freedom of association issues. At the end of the day, we would contend democracy functions better when parties and candidates compete to win the allegiance and votes of eligible voters, not when they compete to shape the electorate to their liking.

Having said that, it is not clear to us what the optimal ballot design should be. In terms of facilitating voting, the straight-ticket option allows committed partisans to efficiently complete the partisan portion of the ballot and minimizes the opportunities for errors and mistakes. It also likely induces people to cast ballots in races that they otherwise would not choose to make a choice in. Our research has shown that in the contemporary era, straight-ticket voting is particularly popular in densely populated urban areas that contain large non-white populations. These areas are subject to crowding and long lines on election day, so the

6.4 Policy Implications: Designing a Better Ballot

straight-ticket option reduces the costs of voting for many voters. At the same time, the results in Chapter 4 suggest that the absence of a party box may enhance legislative responsiveness and legislative effectiveness among legislators. Similar trade-offs are involved with the office bloc versus party column distinction. We are thus reminded that any set of electoral institutions will force us to make trade-offs in areas that may be inconsistent with democratic values (Arrow 1951).

Bibliography

Achen, Christopher H., and Larry M. Bartels. 2017. *Democracy for Realists: Why Elections Do Not Produce Responsive Government*. Princeton, NJ: Princeton University Press.
Adler, E. Scott, and John D. Wilkerson. 2013. *Congress and the Politics of Problem Solving*. Cambridge, UK: Cambridge University Press.
Aidt, Toke, and Peter Jensen. 2017. "From Open to Secret Ballot: Vote Buying and Modernization." *Comparative Political Studies* 50:555–593.
Albright, Spencer D. 1942. *The American Ballot*. Washington, DC: American Council on Public Affairs.
Aldrich, John H. 1993. "Rational Choice and Turnout." *American Journal of Political Science* 37:246–278.
Aldrich, John H. 1995. *Why Parties? The Origin and Transformation of Party Politics in America*. Chicago, IL: University of Chicago Press.
Aldrich, John H., and John D. Griffin. 2017. *Why Parties Matter: Political Competition and Democracy in the American South*. Chicago, IL: University of Chicago Press.
Ansolabehere, Stephen, and Charles Stewart, III. 2015. "Waiting to Vote." *Election Law Journal* 14:47–53.
Anzia, Sarah F. 2012. "Partisan Power Play: The Origins of Local Election Timing as an American Political Institution." *Studies in American Political Development* 26:24–49.
Anzia, Sarah F. 2014. *Timing and Turnout: How Off-Cycle Elections Favor Organized Groups*. Chicago, IL: University of Chicago Press.
Argersinger, Peter H. 1992. *Structure, Process, and Party: Essays in American Political History*. Armonk, NY: M. E. Sharpe.
Arrow, Kenneth J. 1951. *Social Choice and Individual Values*. New York: Wiley and Sons.
Barnes, Tiffany D., Carolina Tchintian, and Santiago Alles. 2017. "Assessing Ballot Structure and Split Ticket Voting: Evidence from a Quasi-Experiment." *Journal of Politics* 79:439–455.

Bawn, Kathleen. 1993. "The Logic of Institutional Preferences: German Electoral Law as a Social Choice Outcome." *American Journal of Political Science* 37:965–989.

Benoit, Kenneth. 2004. "Models of Electoral System Change." *Electoral Studies* 23:363–389.

Bensel, Richard. 2004. *The American Ballot Box in the Mid-Nineteenth Century*. New York: Cambridge University Press.

Bernhard, William, and Tracy Sulkin. 2018. *Legislative Style*. Chicago, IL: University of Chicago Press.

Boix, Carlos. 1999. "Setting the Rules of the Game: The Choice of Electoral Systems in Advanced Democracies." *American Political Science Review* 93:609–624.

Bond, Jon R., and Richard Fleisher. 1990. *The President in the Legislative Arena*. Chicago, IL: University of Chicago Press.

Bourdain, Anthony. 2000. *Kitchen Confidential: Adventures in the Culinary Underbelly*. New York: Bloomsbury.

Brady, Henry E., and John E. McNulty. 2011. "Turning Out to Vote: The Costs of Finding and Getting to the Polling Place." *American Political Science Review* 105:1–20.

Burden, Barry C., and David C. Kimball. 2002. *Why Americans Split Their Tickets: Campaigns, Competition, and Divided Government*. Ann Arbor, MI: University of Michigan Press.

Burden, Barry C., David T. Canon, Kenneth R. Mayer, and Donald P. Moynihan. 2014. "Election Laws, Mobilization, and Turnout: The Unanticipated Consequences of Election Reform." *American Journal of Political Science* 58:95–109.

Cain, Bruce, John Ferejohn, and Morris P. Fiorina. 1987. *The Personal Vote*. Cambridge, MA: Harvard University Press.

Callcott, George H. 1986. *Maryland Political Behavior: Four Centuries of Political Culture*. Baltimore, MD: Maryland Historical Society.

Calvo, Ernesto, Marcelo Escolar, and Julia Pomeres. 2009. "Ballot Design and Split Ticket Voting in Multiparty Systems: Experimental Evidence on Information Effects and Vote Choice." *Electoral Studies* 28:218–231.

Campbell, Angus, and Warren E. Miller. 1957. "The Motivational Basis of Straight and Split Ticket Voting." *American Journal of Political Science* 51(2):293–312.

Campbell, Angus, Phillip E. Converse, Warren E. Miller, and Donald E. Stokes. 1960. *The American Voter*. Chicago, IL: University of Chicago Press.

Canes-Wrone, Brandice, David W. Brady, and John F. Cogan. 2002. "Out of Step, Out of Office: Electoral Accountability and House Members' Voting." *American Political Science Review* 96(1):127–140.

Carey, John M., and Matthew S. Shugart. 1995. "Incentives to Cultivate a Personal Vote: A Rank Ordering of Electoral Formulas." *Electoral Studies* 14:417–439.

Caro, Robert A. 1982. *The Years of Lyndon Johnson: The Path to Power*. New York: Alfred A. Knopf.

Carson, Jamie L., Erik J. Engstrom, and Jason M. Roberts. 2007. "Candidate Quality, the Personal Vote, and the Incumbency Advantage in Congress." *American Political Science Review* 101(2):289–301.

Carson, Jamie L., Gregory Koger, Matthew Lebo, and Everett Young. 2010. "The Electoral Costs of Party Loyalty in Congress." *American Journal of Political Science* 54(3):598–616.

Carson, Jamie L., and Jason M. Roberts. 2013. *Ambition, Competition, and Electoral Reform: The Politics of Congressional Elections Across Time.* Ann Arbor, MI: University of Michigan Press.

Carson, Jamie L., and Joel Sievert. 2015. "Electoral Reform and Changes in Legislative Behavior: Adoption of the Secret Ballot in Congressional Elections." *Legislative Studies Quarterly* 40:83–110.

Converse, Phillip E. 1964. "The Nature of Belief Systems in Mass Publics." In *Ideology and Its Discontents* (David E. Apter, editor), New York: Free Press.

Corder, Kevin J., and Christina Wolbrecht. 2016. *Counting Women's Ballots: Female Voters from Suffrage Through the New Deal.* Cambridge, UK: Cambridge University Press.

Cox, Gary W. 1987. *The Efficient Secret: The Cabinet and the Development of Political Parties in Victorian England.* Cambridge, UK: Cambridge University Press.

Cox, Gary W., and Jonathan N. Katz. 1996. "Why Did the Incumbency Advantage in U.S. House Elections Grow?" *American Journal of Political Science* 40(2):478–497.

Cox, Gary W., and Jonathan N. Katz. 2002. *Elbridge Gerry's Salamander: The Electoral Conseqences of the Reapportionment Revolution.* Cambridge: Cambridge University Press.

Cox, Gary W., and J. Morgan Kousser. 1981. "Turnout and Rural Corruption: New York as a Test Case." *American Journal of Political Science* 25(4):646–663.

Cox, Gary W., and Mathew D. McCubbins. 1993. *Legislative Leviathan: Party Government in the House.* Berkeley, CA: University of California Press.

Cox, Gary W., and Mathew D. McCubbins. 2005. *Setting the Agenda: Responsible Party Government in the U.S. House of Representatives.* Cambridge: Cambridge University Press.

Downs, Anthony. 1957. *An Economic Theory of Democracy.* New York: Harper.

Edwards, George. 1990. *At the Margins: Presidential Leadership of Congress.* New Haven, CT: Yale University Press.

Engstrom, Erik J. 2012. "The Rise and Decline of Turnout in Congressional Elections: Electoral Institutions, Competition, and Strategic Mobilization." *American Journal of Political Science* 56:373–386.

Engstrom, Erik J. 2013. *Partisan Gerrymandering and the Construction of American Democracy.* Ann Arbor, MI: University of Michigan Press.

Engstrom, Erik J., and Samuel Kernell. 2014. *Party Ballots, Reform, and the Transformation of America's Electoral System.* Cambridge, UK: Cambridge University Press.

Erikson, Robert S. 1971. "The Advantage of Incumbency in Congressional Elections." *Polity* 3(3):395–405.

Fredman, L. E. 1968. *The Australian Ballot: The Story of an American Reform.* East Lansing: Michigan State University Press.

Gingerich, Daniel W. 2019. "Ballot Reform as Suffrage Restriction: Evidence from Brazil's Second Republic." *American Journal of Political Science* 63:920–935.

Gingerich, Daniel W., and Luis Fernando Medina. 2013. "The Endurance and Eclipse of the Controlled Vote: A Formal Model of Vote Brokerage under the Secret Ballot." *Economics and Politics* 25:453–480.

Harvey, Anna. 1998. *Votes Without Leverage: Women in American Electoral Politics, 1920–1970.* Cambridge, UK: Cambridge University Press.

Heckelman, Jac. 1995. "The Effect of the Secret Ballot on Voter Turnout Rates." *Public Choice* 82:107–124.

Herrnson, Paul, Michael Hanmer, and Richard Niemi. 2012. "The Impact of Ballot Type on Voter Errors." *American Journal of Political Science* 56:716–730.

Hetherington, Marc J. 2001. "Resurgent Mass Partisanship: The Role of Elite Polarization." *American Political Science Review* 95(03): 619–631.

Hichborn, Franklin. 1909. *Story of the Session of the California Legislature of 1909.* San Francisco, CA: The Press of the James H. Barry Company.

Hichborn, Franklin. 1911. *Story of the Session of the California Legislature of 1911.* San Francisco, CA: The Press of the James H. Barry Company.

Ho, Daniel E., and Kosuke Imai. 2008. "Estimating Causal Effects of Ballot Order from a Randomized Natural Experiment: California Alphabet Lottery, 1978–2002." *Public Opinion Quarterly* 72:216–240.

Hutchinson, W.H. 1969. "Southern Pacific: Myth and Reality." *California Historical Society Quarterly* 48:325–334.

Iacus, Stefano, Gary King, and Giuseppe Porro. 2012. "Causal Inference without Balance Checking: Coarsened Exact Matching." *Political Analysis* 20:1–24.

Jacobson, Gary C. 2015. "It's Nothing Personal: The Decline of the Incumbency Advantage in US House Elections." *Journal of Politics* 77(3):861–873.

Kam, Christopher. 2017. "The Secret Ballot and Market for Votes at 19th Century British Elections." *Comparative Political Studies* 50:594–635.

Katz, Gabriel, R. Michael Alvarez, Ernesto Calvo, Marcelo Escolar, and Julia Pomeres. 2011. "Assessing the Impact of Alternative Voting Technologies on Multi-Party Elections: Design Features, Heuristic Processing, and Voter Choice." *Political Behavior* 33:247–270.

Katz, Jonathan N., and Brian R. Sala. 1996. "Careerism, Committee Assignments, and the Electoral Connection." *American Political Science Review* 90(1):21–33.

Kernell, Samuel. 1997. *Going Public: New Strategies of Presidential Leadership.* Washington, DC: CQ Press.

Key, V. O. 1952. *Politics, Parties, and Pressure Groups.* New York: Ty Crowell Co.

Keyssar, Alexander. 2000. *The Right to Vote: The Contested History of Democracy in the United States.* New York: Basic Books.

Kimball, David C., and Martha Kropf. 2005. "Ballot Design and Unrecorded Votes on Paper-Based Ballots." *Public Opinion Quarterly* 69:508–529.

Koppell, Jonathan GS, and Jennifer A. Steen. 2004. "The Effects of Ballot Position on Election Outcomes." *Journal of Politics* 66:267–281.

Kousser, J. Morgan. 1974. *The Shaping of Southern Politics*. New Haven, CT: Yale University Press.

Lee, Frances. 2016. *Insecure Majorities: Congress and the Perpetual Campaign*. Chicago, IL: University of Chicago Press.

Levendusky, Matthew. 2009. *The Partisan Sort: How Liberals Became Democrats and Conservatives Became Republicans*. Chicago: University of Chicago Press.

Ludington, Arthur C. 1911. *American Ballot Laws, 1888-1910*. University of the State of New York, Albany: New York State Education Department, Bulletin 488.

Lupia, Arthur, and Mathew D. McCubbins. 1998. *The Democratic Dilemma: Can Citizens Learn What They Need to Know?*. Cambridge, UK: Cambridge University Press.

MacKenzie, Scott A. 2015. "Life Before Congress; Using Pre-Congressional Experience to Assess Competing Explanations for Political Professionalism." *Journal of Politics* 77:505–518.

Mares, Isabela. 2015. *From Open Secrets to Secret Voting: Democratic Electoral Reforms and Voter Autonomy*. Cambridge, UK: Cambridge University Press.

Mares, Isabela, and Lauren Young. 2016. "Buying, Expropriating, and Stealing Votes." *Annual Review of Political Science* 19:267–288.

Mayhew, David R. 1974. *Congress: The Electoral Connection*. New Haven: Yale University Press.

McConnaughy, Corrine M. 2015. *The Woman Suffrage Movement in America: A Reassessment*. Cambridge, UK: Cambridge University Press.

Merriam, Charles E., and Louise Overacker. 1928. *Primary Elections*. Chicago IL: University of Chicago Press.

Miller, Joanne M., and Jon A. Krosnick. 1998. "The Impact of Candidate Name Order on Election Outcomes." *Public Opinion Quarterly* 62:291–330.

Nichter, Simeon. 2008. "Vote Buying or Turnout Buying? Machine Politics and the Secret Ballot." *American Political Science Review* 102:19–31.

Niemi, Richard G. 1976. "Costs of Voting and Nonvoting." *Public Choice* 27:115–119.

Nyhan, Brendan, Eric McGhee, John Sides, Seth Masket, and Steven Greene. 2012. "One Vote Out of Step? The Effects of Salient Roll Call Votes in the 2010 Election." *American Politics Research* 40(5):844–879.

Pachon, Monica, Royce Carroll, and Hernando Barragan. 2017. "Ballot Design and Invalid Votes: Evidence from Columbia." *Electoral Studies* 48:98–110.

Patterson, James T. 1972. *Mr. Republican: A Biography of Robert A. Taft*. New York: Houghton Mifflin Company.

Petersen, Eric Falk. 1969. *Prelude to Progressivism: California Election Reform, 1870–1909*. Ph.D. thesis, University of California – Los Angeles.

Polsby, Nelson. 1968. "The Institutionalization of the U.S. House of Representatives." *American Political Science Review* 62(1):144–168.

Reynolds, John F. 2006. *The Demise of the American Convention System, 1880–1911*. New York: Cambridge University Press.

Reynolds, John F., and Richard L. McCormick. 1986. "Outlawing 'Treachery': Split Tickets and Ballot Laws in New York and New Jersey, 1880–1910." *The Journal of American History* 72(4):835–858.

Riker, William H. 1986. *The Art of Political Manipulation*. New Haven, CT: Yale University Press.

Roberts, Jason M., and Jamie L. Carson. 2011. "House and Senate Elections." In *Oxford Handbook of Congress* (Frances Lee, and Eric Schickler, editors), Oxford, UK: Oxford University Press.

Rohde, David W. 1991. *Parties and Leaders in the Postreform House*. Chicago, IL: University of Chicago Press.

Rose, Gary L. 1992. *Connecticut Politics at the Crossroads*. New York: University Press of America.

Rosenstone, Steven, and John Mark Hansen. 1993. *Mobilization, Participation, and Democracy in America*. New York: Macmillan.

Rusk, Jerrold G. 1970. "The Effect of the Australian Ballot Reform on Split Ticket Voting: 1876-1908." *American Political Science Review* 64(4):1220–1238.

Rusk, Jerrold G. 2001. *A Statistical History of the American Electorate*. Washington, DC: Congressional Quarterly Press.

Schickler, Eric. 2001. *Disjointed Pluralism: Institutional Innovation and the Development of the U.S. Congress*. Princeton, NJ: Princeton University Press.

Shepsle, Kenneth A. 2003. "Losers in Politics (and How They Sometimes Become Winners): William Riker's Heresthetic." *Perspectives on Politics* 1:307–315.

Sinclair, Betsy, and R. Michael Alvarez. 2004. "Who Overvotes, Who Undervotes, Using Punchcards? Evidence from Los Angeles County." *Political Research Quarterly* 57:15–25.

Smith, Steven S., and Thomas F. Remington. 2001. *The Politics of Institutional Choice: The Formation of the Russian State Duma*. Princeton, NJ: Princeton University Press.

Smith, Steven S., Jason M. Roberts, and Ryan Vander Wielen. 2013. *The American Congress*. New York: Cambridge University Press, 8th edition.

Sniderman, Paul. 2017. *The Democratic Faith: Essays on Democratic Citizenship*. New Haven, CT: Yale University Press.

Spencer, Douglas M., and Zachary S. Markovits. 2010. "Long Lines at Polling Stations? Observations from an Election Day Field Study." *Election Law Journal* 9:3–17.

Springer, Melanie J. 2014. *American Electoral Institutions and Voter Turnout, 1920–2000*. Chicago, IL: University of Chicago Press.

Stewart III, Charles. 2011. "Voting Technology." *Annual Review of Political Science* 14:353–378.

Stewart III, Charles. 2015. "Managing Polling Place Resources." Caltech/MIT Voting Technology Project.

Stokes, Susan C., Thad Dunning, Marcelo Nazareno, and Valeria Brusco. 2013. *Brokers, Voters, and Clientelism*. Cambridge, UK: Cambridge University Press.

Sulkin, Tracy. 2005. *Issue Politics in Congress*. Cambridge, UK: Cambridge University Press.

Sulkin, Tracy. 2011. *The Legislative Legacy of Congressional Campaigns*. Cambridge, UK: Cambridge University Press.

Summers, Mark Wahlgren. 2004. *Party Games: Getting, Keeping, and Using Power in Gilded Age Politics*. Chapel Hill: University of North Carolina Press.

Taylor, Jeffrey A., Paul S. Herrnson, and James M. Curry. 2018. "The Impact of District Magnitude on the Legislative Behavior of State Representatives." *Political Research Quarterly* 71:302–317.

Thaler, Richard H., and Cass R. Sunstein. 2008. *Nudge: Improving Decisions About Health, Wealth, and Happiness*. New York: Penguin Books.

Thomas, Scott, and Bernard Grofman. 1993. "The Effect of Congressional Rules about Bill Sponsorship on Duplicate Bills: Changing Incentives for Credit Claiming." *Public Choice* 75:93–98.

Valelly, Richard. 2009. *The Two Reconstructions: The Struggle for Black Enfranchisement*. Chicago, IL: University of Chicago Press.

Volden, Craig, and Alan E. Wiseman. 2014. *Legislative Effectiveness in the United States Congress: The Lawmakers*. Cambridge, UK: Cambridge University Press.

Walker, Jack L. 1966. "Ballot Forms and Voter Fatigue: An Analysis of the Office Block and Party Column Ballots." *Midwest Journal of Political Science* 10(4):448–463.

Walsh, Justin E. 1987. *The Centennial History of the Indiana General Assembly, 1816-1978*. Indianapolis, IN: Indiana Historical Bureau.

Wand, Jonathan N., Kenneth W. Shotts, Jasjeet S. Sekhon, Walter R. Mebane, Michael C. Herron, and Henry E. Brady. 2001. "The Butterfly Did It: The Aberrant Vote for Buchanan in Palm Beach County, Florida." *American Political Science Review* 95:793–810.

Ware, Alan. 2002. *The American Direct Primary: Party Institutionalization and Transformation in the North*. New York: Cambridge University Press.

Wawro, Gregory J. 2010. *Legislative Entrepreneurship in the U.S. House of Representatives*. Ann Arbor, MI: University of Michigan Press.

Wigmore, John Henry. 1889. *The Australian Ballot System as Embodied in the Legislation of Various Countries*. Boston, MA: Boston Book Company.

Williams, Hal R. 1973. *The Democratic Party and California Politics, 1880-1896*. Palo Alto, CA: Stanford University Press.

Wittrock, Jill N., Stephen C. Nemeth, Howard Sanborn, Brian DiSarro, and Peverill Squire. 2008. "The Impact of the Australian Ballot on Member Behavior in the U.S. House of Representatives." *Political Research Quarterly* 61:434–444.

Index

2000 Presidential Election, 17, 92–95
  Bush v. Gore, 13, 94
2016 General Election, 104

Alabama, 18, 21
Anglin, Chris, 120

Ballot roll-off, 2, 12, 15, 28–29, 35, 38, 47–49, 52, 53, 55–58, 66–69, 71, 73, 106, 107, 110, 111, 113, 120, 121, 123–128, 131–133
Ballot type, 70, 73, 76, 84, 85, 88
  Australian, 1, 4, 9, 12, 13, 25, 27, 31, 32, 37–43, 48–50, 56–58, 61, 65, 69, 97, 108
  butterfly, 17, 18, 34, 93–94
  lever, 65–69
  office bloc, 6, 12, 13, 15, 24, 25, 28–34, 37, 38, 43, 45, 47–58, 61, 62, 71–76, 79, 81–83, 85, 87–90, 123, 125, 131–133, 136, 141
  party, 12, 15, 30, 38, 39, 43, 73, 75
  party box, 6, 12, 13, 23, 25, 29, 53–55, 58, 69, 71, 75, 76, 79, 81–83, 85, 88, 89, 97–100, 102, 103, 110, 122, 125, 141
  party circle, 44, 46, 47, 134
  party column, 6, 12, 15, 24, 25, 27, 28, 30–32, 37, 43, 45, 46, 48–57, 61, 65, 69, 72, 73, 75, 76, 79, 81–83, 85, 88–90, 122, 125, 131, 133, 135, 136, 141
Barry, James H., 45

Blaine, James G., 41
Brock, Alex, 70
Bryan, William Jennings, 32, 51, 52
Buchanan, Pat, 17, 94
Bush, George H. W., 68
Bush, George W., 12, 17, 18, 92–94
Bush, Jeb, 92

California, 12, 23, 29, 33, 38, 43–48, 53, 133, 139, 140
  Sacramento, 44
  San Francisco, 44, 47
  San Francisco Star, 45
Cannon, Joseph, 59
Carter, Jimmy, 70
Cheney, Dick, 18
Clinton, Bill, 87
Clinton, Chelsea, 87
Colorado, 139
Connecticut, 13, 65–69, 71, 90
Cooper, Roy, 3, 119
Corruption, 39, 40
Cotter, Kevin, 102

Dana, Richard Henry III, 39
DeVos, Betsy, 35, 100, 101, 103

EAC, 98
Earls, Anita, 120
Early voting, 1, 5, 114
Edmunds, Bob, 117–119
Election laws, 30–34, 62, 66, 69, 95–98, 108, 119, 123, 125, 127

149

NAACP v. McCrory, 2
Shelby County v. Holder, 1, 138
secure no-excuse absentee voting (SNRAV), 101–104
Voter Information Verification Act, 1
Voting Rights Act, 1, 2, 104, 107, 138, 139
Weiser Bill, 103

Ferguson, Joseph, 63
Florida, 13, 92–94
　Palm Beach County, 17, 18, 34, 93–94

Gilded Age, 39
Gladstone, Louis I., 66
Gore, Al, 12, 17, 18, 92–94
Gorman, Arthur Pue, 51

Hagan, Kay, 111
Help America Vote Act (HAVA), 13, 31, 33, 94, 95
Hichborn, Franklin, 46
Hill, David Bennet, 34, 35, 48
Hoover, Herbert, 70
Humphrey, Hubert H., 69

Incumbency advantage, 13, 22, 29–30, 60, 63, 71, 73–80, 90, 95, 134, 136
　direct effect, 74, 75
　quality effect, 75, 76
Indiana, 39
Iowa, 14, 122–125
　Osceola County, 123
　Sioux County, 123

Jackson, Barbara, 120
Johnson, Hiram, 33, 47, 133
Johnson, Lyndon, 70, 87, 97
Jones, Doug, 18

Kellems, Vivien, 66
Kentucky, 39

Lausche, Frank J., 62, 65
Lieberman, Joe, 18, 68
Lyons, Lisa Posthumous, 101–103

Margolies-Mezvinsky, Marjorie, 87
Maryland, 12, 25, 32, 38, 49–53, 58, 133
　Baltimore, 51
Massachusetts, 31, 34, 39

McCrory, Pat, 1, 3
McGovern, George, 69
Media markets, 118
Meekof, Arlan, 100–102
Mezvinsky, Marc, 87
Michigan, 6, 14, 34, 35, 96–108, 120–121, 130, 131, 134
　Kent County, 101
　Michigan Supreme Court, 99
　Supreme Court
　　Michigan State A. Philip Randolph Institute, Common Cause, Mary Lansdown, Erin Comartin, and Dion Williams vs. Ruth Johnson, 100, 104
　　Michigan United Conservation Clubs v. Secretary of State, 98
　Wayne County, 103
Missouri, 43
Moore, Roy, 18
Morgan, Mike, 117–119

New Jersey, 41, 42
New York, 12, 34, 38, 39, 41, 42, 48–49, 53, 58, 133
　New York City, 23
Nixon, Richard, 69, 70
North Carolina, 1–4, 6, 13, 14, 29, 34, 69–71, 90, 108–121, 130, 132, 134, 139
　Alleghany County, 2
　Buncombe County, 4
　Camden County, 118
　Cherokee County, 118
　Clay County, 118
　Currituck County, 118
　Durham County, 119
　Edgecombe County, 2
　Orange County, 119
　Supreme Court, 23, 117–120

Obama, Barack, 3, 23, 70, 103, 110, 117, 119, 121
Ohio, 13, 61–65, 71, 74, 90
　Cuyahoga County, 65
Oregon, 139

Panama, 47
Participation, 99
Pew Charitable Trust, 113
Pickrel, William, 62

Index

Polling place wait time, 3, 16, 29, 35, 97, 98, 102, 111–113, 123, 132

Reagan, Ronald, 87
Reichstag, 20
Representational style, 80
  bill sponsorship, 82–83, 90
  credit claiming, 85
  effectiveness, 83–86, 90, 141
  roll-call voting, 86–88, 90
Roebuck, Justin, 102
Romano, Mike, 125
Romney McDaniel, Ronna, 35, 102–103
Romney, Mitt, 3
Roosevelt, Franklin D., 62, 87
Roosevelt, Theodore, 46
Rouse, Frank, 70

Snyder, Rick, 102
South Dakota, 43
Southern Pacific Company, 33, 44–46
Stanford, Leland, 44
Straight-ticket voting, 1–3, 6, 11, 14, 15, 23, 24, 28, 35, 37, 43–45, 47, 49–52, 55–57, 61–63, 65, 68, 69, 72, 74, 79, 81, 90, 96, 98–100, 103–105, 108, 110–115, 117, 120, 121, 123–128, 130–136, 139–141

Taft, Robert A., 62–65, 68, 74, 76
Texas, 92, 96
Tillis, Thom, 111
Trump, Donald, 123, 124
Turnout, 2, 3, 10, 12, 14, 38, 40, 57, 58, 95, 113–115, 121, 132

United States Senate, 44, 51
  Finance Committee, 62
  Labor and Public Welfare Committee, 62

Voter demographics, 2, 28, 29, 51, 114, 115, 117, 119, 121, 125, 132, 140
  African American, 2, 25, 29, 32, 36, 98, 99, 104, 109, 110, 112, 114, 121, 132, 134, 138, 139

Wallace, George, 70
Weicker, Lowell, 68, 69
Weiser, Ron, 103, 104
West Virginia, 14, 125–127
Williams, Pat, 87
Wilson, Woodrow, 49

Yelton, Don, 4

Zaagman, Bill, 102

Lightning Source UK Ltd.
Milton Keynes UK
UKHW010652040722
405333UK00008B/135